Edward Hay
HISTORIAN OF 1798

Edward Hay

HISTORIAN OF 1798

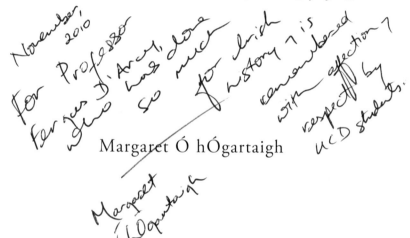

November, 2010

For Professor Fergus D'Arcy, who has done so much for Irish history ~ is remembered with affection ~ respect by UCD students.

Margaret Ó hÓgartaigh

Margaret Ó hÓgartaigh

The History Press Ireland

For Tom Bartlett and Ciara Breathnach

First published 2010

The History Press Ireland
119 Lower Baggot Street
Dublin 2, Ireland
www.thehistorypress.ie

British Library Cataloguing in Publication Data.
A catalogue record for this book is available from the British Library.

ISBN 978 1 84588 992 0

Typesetting and origination by The History Press
Printed in Great Britain
Manufacturing managed by Jellyfish Print Solutions Ltd

CONTENTS

❧

ACKNOWLEDGEMENTS

My thanks to Louis Cullen, whose seminars in Trinity College Dublin were consistently stimulating. Kevin Whelan was a mine of information on the Hays and Wexford. Margaret and John Maher in Ballinkeele House, Wexford were gracious and hospitable. Philomena Hughes and Marie Hay, provided the painting of Edward Hay; Mary Rose Hay and Vincent Hay, direct descendants of Edward Hay, provided me with new documentary evidence on the Hay family. I am grateful for their generosity. Bill Sweetman, a direct descendant of Edward's Hay's first cousin, was also generous with his research.

I am grateful to various librarians and archivists: John Kirwan, St Kieran's College, Kilkenny; Colette O'Daly, National Library of Ireland; Bernadette Cunningham, Royal Irish Academy; Marie Boran, National University of Ireland, Galway; Heather Stanley, Public Record Office of Northern Ireland; Catherine O'Rourke, formerly Wexford County Library; Brian Donnelly, National Archives of Ireland; Niamh O'Sullivan, Kilmainham Gaol; Benjamin Longden, Sheffield City Archives, and the staff at the Trinity College, Dublin, Early Printed Books and the Manuscripts Department. I am grateful to the Wentworth Woodhouse Muniments and Sheffield City Council for permission to quote from the Fitzwilliam papers in their archives. David Sheehy, formerly Dublin Diocesan Archivist, was always willing and able to respond to my varied requests. I am indebted to the multilingual archivists at the Propaganda Fide Archives in Rome.

Belated thanks to Clare County Council, who helped fund my undergraduate education at the National University of Ireland, Galway, and to Tom Bartlett, Nicholas Canny, Steve Ellis, Daibhí Ó Croinin and Gearóid Ó Tuathaigh, as well as the late Gearóid

MacNiocaill and Tom O'Neill, who all taught me history in an accessible and scholarly manner at NUIG. My belated thanks to Niall Ó Ciosain for his many kindnesses.

Fergus D'Arcy, Ray Gillespie, Jimmy Kelly and Kevin Whelan encouraged me to publish this book. Sean Connolly kindly commented on my earlier work on Edward Hay. Gillian O'Brien and Lindsey Earner-Byrne made perceptive suggestions. Marie Boran, Caitriona Clear, Mary Teresa Moran, Bernadette Prendergast, Martina Naughton, Celestine Rafferty, Dáire Keogh, Tommy Graham, Nicky Furlong, Bernard Browne, Joe Bishop, Mary Bishop and Seamus De Bhál helped me with my research, as did Teresa Wilson and Jean Whelan, who provided accommodation during research trips to Dublin and Wexford. Jim Whelan encouraged the pursuit of research. Ailish O'Brien's support sustained me. Marianne Elliott kindly agreed to write a foreword. My greatest debt is in the dedication. Ciara Breathnach was engaging, illuminating and insightful. Tom Bartlett introduced me to the elegance of the eighteenth century and, through his advice and encouragement, gave my earlier work on Edward Hay the scholarly rigour it required. I am very grateful to all at The History Press, especially Maeve Convery and Ronan Colgan. Finally, thanks to Ciarán for everything.

Margaret Ó hÓgartaigh,
Blackrock, Dublin.

ABOUT THE AUTHOR

Dr Margaret Ó hÓgartaigh works at All Hallows, Dublin City University and is a Fellow of the Royal Academy of Medicine in Ireland. She was a Fulbright Fellow at Boston College and is the author of *Kathleen Lynn: Irishwoman, Patriot, Doctor* (2006) and, with Ciarán Ó hÓgartaigh, *Business Archival Sources for the Local Historian* (2010).

FOREWORD

The name of Edward Hay does not figure prominently in popular imagination, yet his tireless work for Catholic emancipation, from the 1790s to the 1820s, helped make Daniel O'Connell's success possible. Margaret Ó hÓgartaigh's book about his life and that of his family also tells us much about how the Catholic gentry coped with restrictions under the Penal Laws. It is particularly vivid in the light it throws on the history of Wexford during the 1798 Rebellion. So influential was Hay's History of the Wexford rebellion, written in 1803, that it skewed historical understanding for nearly two centuries. Here Margaret Ó hÓgartaigh disentangles fact from myth and reveals much of the highly ambiguous role that Edward Hay played in the rebellion. Along the way she has provided considerable new evidence of the criss-crossing of personal relationships in Wexford, which defied the stereotypical Catholic–Protestant polarisation.

Having survived the rebellion, Hay then became pivotal to the post-Union Catholic campaign, which he bankrolled when subscriptions dwindled, much to his own and his family's impoverishment. This book adds significantly to our knowledge of the long and frustrating campaign before the success of 1829. Sadly, Hay died in somewhat tragic circumstances three years short of that victory.

He was not the easiest person to deal with, but his sheer doggedness and many his sacrifices in the campaign ought to have secured him greater recognition than he has had to date. Margaret Ó hÓgartaigh deserves much credit for bringing him out of the shadows in this very comprehensive book about the life and work of one of Ireland's unsung champions.

Marianne Elliott,
September 2010

I

WEXFORD, 1760-89

Edward Hay (*c*.1761-1826) was born into a Wexford, Catholic, landed family. His early life and education abroad were typical of wealthy Catholics during the eighteenth century.[1] However, Hay's involvement in the radical politics of the 1790s, his role in the Rebellion of 1798 and his *History* of the event, as well as his heavy involvement in Catholic organisations after the Act of Union, set him apart from many of his contemporaries.

This book will discuss Hay's impact on Catholic politics between 1792 and 1822. Hay was unusual in his long-term involvement with Catholic politics. His political career spanned over thirty years. During his lifetime, Ireland's Catholics emerged from the restrictions of the Penal Laws and they achieved emancipation three years after his death. Hay's generation spanned the era from political exclusion to mass mobilisation of Irish Catholics. This book is not a history of Catholic politics before the achievement of emancipation. Rather, it is a political biography of one of the more important, yet over-looked, activists of the era.

Initially this book examines the background to the Catholic question in Ireland and Hay's early life in Wexford and on the continent between 1760 and 1790. Hay's activities during the crisis-ridden 1790s and his involvement in the Catholic convention of 1792, the recall of Lord Lieutenant Earl Fitzwilliam in 1795 and, most importantly, the rebellion in Wexford during 1798, will be analysed. His influential *History* of the rebellion will then be examined. The partisan nature of his work and its impact on contemporary and current interpretations of the rebellion is discussed. Hay's work as secretary to the various Catholic bodies between 1807 and 1819 provides the context in which to discuss the growing politicisation of Irish Catholics. Finally, the last years of Hay's life and his attempts to vindicate his work are assessed.

This book concludes with an analysis of Hay's significance. His lengthy involvement in Catholic politics and the views of his contemporaries are suggestive of Hay's prominence in Irish life for three decades. Through Hay, one can discover the inner workings of Catholic politics in the crucial decades before the achievement of emancipation in 1829.

HAY AND THE HISTORIANS

Edward Hay is not a well-known Irish historical figure.[2] Between 1792 and 1822, he was a cornerstone in Catholic affairs which historians have rejected. Most of the information relating to him concerns his activities in the 1790s. Historians Louis Cullen and Kevin Whelan, in their publications on Wexford in the last decade of the eighteenth century, have made much of Hay's involvement in the politics of the period.[3] In the post-Union period, however, when the Catholic question, that is the exclusion of Catholics from parliament, became an increasingly important issue, much less attention has been paid to him. Partial suffrage for Catholics had been obtained in the 1790s, but this did not satisfy radical activists like Hay. Accounts of the period scarcely refer to the long-term secretary of the Irish Catholics. During Hay's lifetime the position of Irish Catholics changed dramatically. He facilitated their transformation.

Edward Hay's precise role in the 1798 Rebellion needs to be carefully analysed. Daniel Gahan's illuminating history of the rebellion in Wexford suggests that Hay 'went about creating an infant armaments departments' at the battle of Vinegar Hill.[4] Tom Dunne's significant meditation on rebellions (both personal and political) makes extensive use of Hay's *History* and emphasises the importance of Hay's account.[5] Kevin Whelan's examination of '98 after '98 illustrates the influence of Hay's work on later historians.[6] Furthermore, the enormous collection of essays on 1798 also refers to Hay's *History*, but there is little on the role he played in the rebellion.[7]

Why, then, has Hay been ignored? The secondary material suggests that he, like many of his contemporaries, was overshadowed by 'The Liberator' Daniel O'Connell.[8] The publication of O'Connell's correspondence has also made possible a better understanding of the development of Catholic politics and the achievement of emancipation.[9] Regrettably, for too long, Catholic activities were viewed

from the standpoint of O'Connell, and other figures such as Denys
Scully, Troy and Hay were ignored. Fortunately, the cataloguing of
the Catholic Association papers (including Hay's voluminous correspondence) at the Dublin Diocesan Archives has made an appraisal
of Hay's role possible.[10] Denys Scully played a very important part
in earlier Catholic organisations, but until the 1980s he, too, was
ignored. The editing of the Scully papers by Brian MacDermot has
rectified this omission by outlining the importance of Scully in the
achievement of Catholic Emancipation.[11] Work by Vincent McNally
and Dáire Keogh have emphasised the importance of John Thomas
Troy (the Catholic Archbishop of Dublin between 1787 and 1823) in
the pursuit of Catholic relief.[12] The influential work on the Catholic
question by Tom Bartlett provides a context for Hay's career.[13]

This book proposes to discuss and assess the importance of Hay's
career as a census-taker, delegate, petitioner, 'reluctant rebel', and,
finally, secretary to various Catholic organisations for over a decade.
At the outset, it is necessary to sketch in the development of the
Catholic question in the first thirty years of Hay's life.

CATHOLIC POLITICS, 1760-1790

The Catholic Committee existed continuously from 1756 until its
dissolution in 1793.[14] It had been established by Charles O'Conor
of Belanagare, County Roscommon, Dr John Curry of Dublin and
Thomas Wyse of Waterford. O'Conor was a well-known antiquarian
and his letters contain useful information on the early years of the
Catholic Committee.[15] Both O'Conor and Curry, a physician, published pamphlets on Catholic relief and tried 'through the medium of
their writings, to break down the prejudices entertained against the
Catholics'.[16] Wyse was well known for his commitment to moderate
political change. However, the Catholic Committee was very inactive
until the 1790s, though it did maintain a theoretical existence.

Furthermore, the reorganisation of the Catholic Church also helped
to push the Catholic question to the forefront of Irish politics. There
was a desire to impose European (Tridentine) structures and organisation on the Irish Catholic Church. The leading bishops, in particular,
were to play an important part in the passing of Catholic Relief Acts
in 1778 and 1782. These Relief Acts must be seen in the light of British
political developments. The penal legislation against those who were

not members of the established Church (*i.e.* the episcopalian Church) was an embarrassment. After all, this was the 'Age of Enlightenment', even if this influential intellectual movement was resolutely anti-Catholic. In Ireland, it was difficult to know how to accommodate the Catholics without alienating the Protestant ascendancy elite in the Irish parliament. It may be argued that, to prevent the Irish parliament becoming too assertive and independent Westminster ultimately agreed to the passing of the Relief Acts. Catholic emancipation was a cause 'embraced as much from opportunism as from enlightenment'.[17] The British government realised the strategic importance of keeping Ireland at peace, particularly during a revolutionary era. British politicians were fearful that the Catholics would align themselves with the revolutionaries of America and, later, France. It has been argued that the Relief Act of 1778 'was largely the product of a policy initiated in London to ensure Catholic loyalty in the event of an invasion'.[18] The involvement of the Catholic Committee in the Relief Acts of 1778 and 1782 was minimal. Dublin Castle was hostile to relief, and the Irish parliament, with a few notable exceptions, was not noted for its liberal views. The Irish parliament at College Green was virtually forced to accept Catholic Relief measures by the British Government. The achievement of legislative independence for the Irish parliament in 1782 did not further the cause of the Catholics. A number of factors affected the progress of the Catholic question in the 1780s and these factors will be discussed in turn.

The activities of rural secret societies, particularly the Whiteboys, had an important impact on events (especially the Catholic question) at a national level. The Whiteboys were active in the 1760s, just as the Catholics began to organise themselves politically. Although their aims were local and agrarian (such as the regulation of tithes paid to the established Church, and other peasant grievances like low wages and unemployment), they also managed to revive Protestant fears about Catholic desires to reverse the land settlements of the seventeenth century. The Whiteboys were seen as the 'champions of the poor' who had no legal redress for their grievances.[19] As 'levellers' in an authoritarian society they were considered socially corrosive and potentially explosive. They fed off rural strife, and among those of their own background they were tolerated. The Catholic Church, however, was very critical of their activities. Additionally, Catholic agitators were fearful of making too many demands for Catholic relief in the face of rural strife. They were also worried lest their agitation was perceived as subversive. The Whiteboys wanted to rectify local and agrarian grievances. They were not politically radical like the Defenders, whose sectarianism particularly affected the lower levels of Irish society in the 1790s.

However, the most significant result of the Whiteboys and the Rightboys of the mid-1780s was the fear they engendered of a 'popish plot'. For example, it was rumoured that Catholics intended to murder all Protestants on Good Friday. The British War (during the 1770s) against two Catholic powers, France and Austria, fed these Protestant fears and provided a justification for the 'No Popery' cry. Catholics who were falsely accused of being members of secret societies (for example Fr Nicholas Sheehy) were brought to trial and punished. These early societies 'helped to establish the tradition of secret societies in Ireland'. The Whiteboys and the Rightboys were the precursors of the Defenders and they were used as an argument against the achievement of Catholic relief since they emphasised the anti-Protestant and, ultimately, sectarian elements in Irish life.[20] 'Rangers', a group that was established to counteract the secret societies, eventually fed into the Volunteers and it is to this latter group that we must now turn.

VOLUNTEERS AND REFORM

Catholic relief was also linked to the Volunteers and the pursuit of parliamentary reform. The Volunteers had been formed in 1778 and they could be described as the military wing of the 'patriot party' whose aim was to achieve legislative independence for the Irish parliament. They had achieved respectability through the support of prominent patriot Members of Parliament such as Henry Grattan and Henry Flood:

> The participation of the Volunteers in the campaigns for free trade, legislative independence and renunciation between 1778 and 1783 had demonstrated the capacity of extra-parliamentary agitation to achieve legislative changes – hence the parliamentary reform movement's resort to the same tactics.[21]

The overwhelmingly conservative Catholic Committee still shied away from extra-parliamentary activities and this tactic led, in part, to a split in the Committee between conservative and radical elements in 1791. Of more relevance to Edward Hay was the fact that Catholics established their own Volunteer corps, but the 'gentlemen of Counties Meath and Wexford refused to associate in arms with' the Volunteers.[22] Hay bemoaned the fact that 'there was no admission for a Catholic among the Volunteers of Wexford'.[23] George Ogle (a loyalist Wexford MP) was resented in Wexford because he had supported the Volunteers, while the independent MP Charles O'Conor criticised 'the patriotic Mr Ogle, who has got a government pension and is now the mouth-piece of the court'.[24] Despite the failure of the Volunteers to wholeheartedly admit Catholics to their ranks, politicians were willing to use the Volunteer agitation in order to further parliamentary reform. Grattan 'exploited the strength of the Volunteer movement' and 'he used and encouraged the Volunteers to act as a political machine'.[25] Unfortunately for the Catholics, the Volunteers acquiesced with the 'anti-popery' mentality of many members of the Ascendancy. The national Volunteer convention held in Dublin during November 1783 refused to discuss the Catholic question. It was the Catholic issue that split the reform campaign.[26]

The Volunteers' greatest significance lies in the impact they had on Anglo-Irish relations. The British parliament realised that its Irish counterpart was willing to show its muscle if parliamentary reform was not forthcoming in the 1780s. Not surprisingly, this worried some politicians. As early as two decades before its enactment, there were discussions about a Union between the two countries. Ironically, the political triumph of the Irish parliament in achieving the Constitution of 1782 destabilised the Irish political structure. The Irish parliament was not trusted by Westminster. It was regarded, at best, as a 'giddy institution' by the conservative MP John Fitzgibbon. Politicians at Westminster realised that the Catholic card could be played in Ireland.

The Catholics, despite their inferior status before the law (though that was now changing), became a much sought after group in the 1780s and '90s. If they could be lured away from the 'Patriot Parliament' (with the promise of legislative relief), then so much the better for Westminster. This would prevent the Irish patriot politicians from becoming too independent. Theobald Wolfe Tone, a young Protestant lawyer, persuasively contended in his pamphlet, 'An argument on behalf of the Catholics of Ireland' (1791), that the Catholics held the balance between Dublin Castle and the Protestants. This argument partly explains why Catholics were courted by the government. If real reform was to be achieved, then the radical Protestants would have to drop their traditional fears about 'popery' and ally themselves with the Catholics. By 1791, the 'race was on for the Catholic soul. Would they throw their weight behind the radical reformers [Tone and the United Irishmen] or would they be won over by government concessions?'[27] The choices facing the Catholics and their responses to these choices explain many of the developments in the 1790s.

Conservative British politicians attempted to lure the Catholics away from radical societies such as the United Irishmen, again with legislative relief as the carrot. The Relief Acts of 1774, 1778 and 1782 had all been initiated by Westminster. By 1790, as a result of these Relief Acts, Catholic religious restrictions were gone. What of the Catholics in the 1770s and 1780s? Many commentators have referred to the rise in Catholic confidence in this period. It related, in part, to the increased economic power enjoyed by Catholics. They were heavily involved in trade and the army, both at home and on the continent. Their wealth was cited as a valid reason for representation in the Irish parliament.[28] The Catholics argued that their prosperity was wasted when they were not able to gain access to the Irish political nation.

Catholic confidence was most evident in the upsurge in chapel building. Places of worship developed from 'Mass-rock to Mass-house to chapel'.[29] In addition to a strong commitment to their faith, Catholics increased their political and social strength through kindred loyalties, which formed a 'web of solidarity' between families. It has been argued that Catholics shared a common identity. This identity:

> …was as much ethnic as religious, and … its force lay more in the emotional and symbolic … than in the actual realm (dispossession affected only a tiny minority of Catholics, legal bars to Catholics impinged only on the professionals). Allegiance to Catholicism became the badge of this historical grudge, and Catholicism became almost a vast trade union representing the shared interests of this dispossessed group.[30]

In the latter half of the eighteenth century, Catholics were no longer willing to endure – they wanted to emerge. The presence of educated and politically aware Catholics changed the face of Irish politics in the 1790s. They were not willing to show deference towards the aristocrats on the Catholic Committee who presumed to speak for the Catholics of Ireland.

The English Catholic Committee, like its Irish counterpart, was divided. In the late 1780s, the revival of English Catholics encouraged their Irish counterparts to push for relief legislation. The English Catholic Committee was established by laymen in 1783. Charles Butler, their secretary, was the leading light on the committee. Although the committee became a very important force, it was dominated by members of the anti-episcopal, Cisalpine club.[31] This naturally led to differences with the hierarchy, particularly Bishop John Milner, vicar apostolic of the Midland district, and an arch-enemy of Butler. Both Milner and Butler were to play an important part in English Catholic politics in the early nineteenth century. The English Catholic Committee provided the impetus for fur-ther Catholic Relief in the 1790s, although by that stage the British parliament was intent on placating Catholics, for fear they would imbibe French revolutionary ideas.

By 1790, the increase in extra-parliamentary activities, growing turbulence in Irish society, the threat of an upsurge in rural unrest, as well as the destabilised political structure, all contributed to a changed atmosphere in Ireland. The Irish Catholic Committee had proved to be a forum for disputes and little else. Who would speak for the Catholics?

This, then, was the Ireland in which Edward Hay spent his form-ative years. However, it is necessary, first of all, to look at the local background of Edward Hay before discussing his family context and early life in Wexford and on the continent.

WEXFORD POLITICS IN THE 1770S AND 1780S

Wexford was a very diverse county in the late eighteenth century. In the 1910s, Robert Lynd, the northern essayist and nationalist, declared that 'Enniscorthy is the Belfast of the south.'[32] Why was this? Land dis-possession in the seventeenth century had left its mark on the county. Catholics predominated in the south of the county while Protestants were dominant in the north. The middle ground was an amalgam of the two. The sectarian demographics of Wexford created ten-sions.[33] Kevin Whelan, who has done extensive research on Wexford in the 1790s, has identified the county as being part of the Catholic 'core area'. The zone stretching from 'Wexford, through Carlow, Kilkenny, Waterford, Tipperary, north and east Cork into Limerick and north Kerry [was the] heartland and powerhouse of modern Irish Catholicism'.[34] Not surprisingly, Wexford was one the more volatile parts of Ireland during the Whiteboy/Rightboy disturbances.

Geographically, of all the counties outside Ulster, Wexford contained the highest proportion of Protestant settlers. The concentration of these settlers in the north of the county ensured that events in Wexford could easily take on a sectarian character. In addition to this, Catholics were dispersed within Protestant settlements. The political divisions in Wexford also lent the county towards sectarianism. There was a well-established Protestant ascendancy party in Wexford. Prominent members of this group included Lord Ely and George Ogle. The anti-Catholicism of this group was a matter of public record. For example, it was well known that Ogle opposed the Catholic Relief Acts.

To complicate matters, there was also a strong liberal party in Wexford. Its leading lights including the Grogan, Colclough and Harvey families. All of these families would be involved in the 1798 Rebellion. The anti-Catholic ascendancy party dominated in the north of the county, while the liberals' main power base was in the south. As Kevin Whelan has argued, these two 'organised electoral power blocks … ensured that all national debates and issues were imported and diffused widely in Wexford, creating a politicised and polarised constituency'. It also meant that 'the political temperature was amongst the hottest in the country' and there were debates on, and divisions over, all issues. As one would expect, the Catholic question created the biggest divisions. Of course, not all Protestants were members of Ogle's ascendancy party. Nonetheless, with the polarisation of Wexford politics, all elections included a sectarian element. Politically these 'lines of cleavage were already well established in the 1770s and had hardened considerably by the 1790s'.[35] The moderate Lord Mountnorris (who was later to work with Hay) was one of the few individuals who tried to maintain good relations with both groups.

Socially, Wexford Catholic families were closely linked, either by blood or through commercial connections. The strength of these 'extended families' was very evident in the 1798 Rebellion. Edward Hay's family background and the kinship networks with other prominent families had an impact on his political outlook.

EDWARD HAY AND WEXFORD, 1760-1789

The Hays were of Norman extraction. They were one of the chief Norman families who arrived in Ireland in the reign of Henry II in the Barony of Forth. The Wexford antiquarian Philip Hore wrote that Richard de Hay, Lord of Hay in Wales, came to Wexford in 1169 with his kinsman Hervey de Montemarisco and obtained grants of land in the Barony of Forth and Bargy.[36] The family name had 'originated in La Hay du Puite in Manche, Normandy'. The Hays were prominent in Wexford from the twelfth century. Richard Hay was one of the witnesses at the foundation charter of Dunbrody Abbey in 1176 and Thomas Hay was a sheriff of Wexford in 1284. Furthermore, the Hays provided four mayors of Wexford.[37] R.R. Madden, the hagiographer of the United Irishmen, gave an account of Hay's genealogy which began in 1418.[38] The Hays, at one stage, owned the 'Towers of Hill, Slade, Tascumshene and Castlehays town'.[39] A local historian has written that the Hay's Hill Castle was as 'powerful in early prestige as the family who occupied it'.[40] The family also served under Charles I and Charles II.[41] Their land was forfeited after the Cromwellian Act of Settlement and the main branch of the Hay family settled at Ballinkeele, about four miles from Enniscorthy, between Ballymurn and Glenbrien.[42] Edward Hay maintained that James II had slept in Ballinkeele during his flight to Duncannon. The Hays maintained their connections with France, since one of the family settled at Nantes and they were part of the nobility in that city.[43] In an article written on Hay, and possibly written by Hay himself, it was claimed that the Hays were 'descended from the celebrated Earls of Errol', but that is the only reference to a Scottish connection among the Hay family.[44]

Hay's father, Harvey, married Catherine Fergus, whose father was from Dublin.[45] Sir Richard Musgrave, a staunch defender of the Protestant ascendancy and polemical historian of the 1798 Rebellion, wrote that the Hays were an 'ancient popish family [and that] Mr Harvey Hay of Ballinkeele [was] noted for his hospitality'.[46] In a less than modest assessment, Edward Hay described his family as 'ancient and respectable', as well as being 'highly respected and esteemed by the most respectable characters of all religious persuasions in Wexford'.[47]

According to Madden, Harvey Hay had four sons, Edward, Philip, John and James, as well as several daughters, whose names we are not told. Apparently, they 'don't count'![48] Harvey Hay was a pioneer in the breeding of racehorses and many of the Hays who fought abroad became cavalry officers.[49] This equine tradition was continued by the Maher family, who bought Ballinkeele House from the Hays in 1825. They produced the Grand National winner in 1889.[50]

There was a tradition of continental education among wealthy Irish Catholics, and the Hays were no different.[51] James and John Hay were educated in Ireland and Austria respectively, and John fought in France as an officer in Dillon's regiment of the Irish Brigade. He returned from France in 1793 and settled in Newcastle near Wexford with his wife, Catherine.[52] James fought for the British army and died in St Lucia in the West Indies in 1796. Philip featured in the English and History prize lists for St Kieran's College, Kilkenny in 1788 and 1789.[53] He was later to have a very successful career in the British army. Hence, two of the Hays, James and Philip, served in the British army. This occupation provided career opportunities for many Irish Catholics. Edward was educated in France and Germany and even Musgrave admitted that Hay was extremely well educated. The impact of the Penal Laws was made clear when Hay lamented that he was 'fully sensible of [his] civil degradation as a Catholic', since he was forced to go to the continent for a full education. This undoubtedly affected his outlook.[54] An article in Watty Cox's *Irish Magazine* maintained that Hay was sent abroad 'at an early age … to receive an education suitable to his respectable line of life, which vandal legislators had denied him at home'. Academically, Hay achieved the success which was 'expected from his natural abilities'. His educational experience affected his view of Catholics in Ireland, where they were inferior before the law. He had been educated in France, where the Catholics were members of the ruling elite. However, he returned to Ireland 'from France, previous to the Revolution', where 'a Catholic was scarcely considered a Human Being'.[55] Hay was 'fully sensible of [his] … degraded state, as a Catholic'.[56] As well as making Catholics aware of their disabilities, Irish connections with Catholic Europe, which were forged by educational and commercial links, helped to build a sense of Catholic solidarity in the late eighteenth century.

Harvey Hay, unlike his son Edward, was prepared to be patient in the pursuit of Catholic emancipation. An 'old-style' Catholic, he believed that a deferential and dutiful approach was the best method of obtaining political concessions. In the 1770s, for example, twenty-eight Wexford Catholics 'took advantage of the repeal of the Penal Laws to signify judicially their loyalty to the British Crown, despite the opposition of Bishop Sweetman'.[57] One of the leading signatories was Harvey Hay. Furthermore, as a result of the links between Catholics in Wexford and Dublin (Wexford gentry such as Mathew Talbot, Robert Devereux, Luke Masterson and Thomas Esmonde were active in the Catholic Committee in the 1780s),[58] Harvey was aware of national developments. Such was the extent of Harvey's prominence and loyalty that, in 1793, he was selected as a Justice of the Peace. He was, in fact, the first Catholic juror for 200 years. Despite this family honour, Edward Hay was acutely aware of the sense of collective grievance among Catholics. His extended family, as well as his background in Wexford, clearly influenced his participation in the politics of the 1790s.

Hay's early life, background and education were typical of many wealthy Catholics in the last quarter of the eighteenth century. A useful comparison with the Hay background is the Sweetman family of Newbawn in County Wexford.[59] Like the Hays, they survived the plantations and resulting upheavals of the seventeenth and eighteenth centuries. Through fishing trade with Newfoundland, the Sweetmans became very wealthy. Their family centre at Newbawn, similar to the Hay residence at Ballinkeele, 'provided the classic background for entry into eighteenth century mercantile trade or a career in the upper echelons of the re-emerging Irish Catholic Church'.[60] Both families, through their wealth and connections, were politically and socially prominent in Wexford. In 1798, the Sweetmans and the Hays were directly or indirectly involved with the United Irishmen. In the early nineteenth century, Nicholas Sweetman was involved in Catholic organisations at a local level.

Hay's early life coincided with the growth in the importance of the Catholic question, both as a local and national issue. The middle-class Catholic families of this period had a 'capacity to generate surplus wealth' and 'an outward looking orientation' helped, no doubt, by a continental education. These families, allied to the increasingly assertive mercantile group, provided much of the leadership for the events of the 1790s. They had links with the centres of European Catholicism through their relations (the Hays in Nantes, for example) or through mercantile links. Given their 'combination of wealth and awareness of the outside world', it was inevitable that these Catholics would, 'in the changed political circumstances of the late eighteenth century, turn [their] attention to legal and political disabilities affecting Irish Catholics'.[61]

Kinship ties, particularly in Wexford, cannot be over emphasised. Kevin Whelan has anatomised the inter-connections between prominent Wexford Catholics in the late eighteenth century. Hay's first cousins Edward Fitzgerald and James Edward Devereux played major roles in the events of the 1790s. The interdependency between these families helped to forge strong loyalties. Some of these loyalties were to be shattered in the 1790s. Nonetheless, Wexford was one of the more important counties for Irish Catholic mobilisation. The dynamic mixture of cultural cohesiveness and surplus wealth led to the creation of an increasingly self-confident and restless Catholic community. Hay was a part of that community. Family ties also helped spread radical ideas, 'These families were frequently intermarried and lines of easy communication existed between them, creating a resilient, tight-knit grouping.'[62] The landed families in Wexford saw themselves, and were seen, as the rightful leaders of the Catholic community, very aware of their origins and former status. They belonged to a Wexford Catholic aristocracy which had its own unifying force and momentum, invigorated by the 'kinship mechanism'. Edward Hay frequently referred to his standing and influence in the community.[63] These families, if they survived, were the backbone of the Catholic organisations in the late eighteenth and early nineteenth centuries. Increasingly assertive Catholicism was also evident from the resurgence in institutional Catholicism. The Hays played host to the parish priest of Ballymurn, and Catholics increasingly gave central locations to their chapels.[64]

On the economic front, Maureen Wall has demonstrated the strength of Catholics in home and foreign trade, and this increased Catholic confidence even further.[65] Commercial and political links with Dublin helped to politicise Catholics in Wexford and they further facilitated the spread of radical ideas, particularly among members of the Catholic Committee. In the 1780s, the Wexford gentry were prominent members of the Catholic Committee. This politicisation of the elite levels of Wexford society inevitably meant Hay and his contemporaries were all too aware of their status as natural leaders and a 'dispossessed elite'.

II

THE MAKING OF A
RADICAL, 1790-98

Hay's career in the 1790s pinpoints the entry of middle and upper-class Catholics into Irish public life. This entry was facilitated by a number of factors. Increased confidence and wealth, as documented in chapter one, encouraged Catholics to become involved in national issues. The Relief Acts of 1778 and 1782 and the crisis in Protestant circles also encouraged Catholic activity during the 1780s and 90s. The early 1790s saw the merging of Wexford and national politics. The attendance of Wexford representatives at Catholic Committee meetings ensured that they were very aware of national issues. An increasingly abrasive attitude and the abandonment of servile approaches were clearly evident among the Wexford representatives. Hay was a prominent member of the Wexford delegation. This chapter will trace the development of Catholic activity in general, and Edward Hay in particular, from the relative peace of the early 1790s, to the explosive events at the end of the decade.

By 1798, Hay had been active in Wexford politics for at least six years. He was, as Kevin Whelan phrased it, along with his contemporary James Edward Devereux, a 'conspicuous public' man and a 'recognised opposition figure'.[66] Devereux and Hay had extensive political experience from earlier events, such as the 1793 Militia Act and the recall of Fitzwilliam in 1795.

Throughout the 1790s, authoritarian discipline was challenged, as Catholics demanded relief as a right and not just a concession. Yet, even if their aspirations were similar, prominent Catholic families did not always share the same views about tactics. Harvey Hay was to become estranged from his eldest son Edward over differences in their pursuit of Catholic emancipation.

A REVOLUTIONARY ERA

The founding of the United Irishmen in 1791 signalled the increasing radicalisation of Irish political life. Ultimately, this proposed 'United Irish' alliance between Catholics and Dissenters (linked as they were in 'a community of insult', to use Thomas Addis Emmet's striking description) did not reach its full potential, partly because the Relief Acts of 1792 and 1793 placated the conservative Catholics. Hay and his radical contemporaries were not satisfied with the limited relief of these acts. The more aggressive Catholics began to make their presence felt on the Catholic Committee. The aristocratic group on the committee, which had usually dictated affairs, led by Lord Kenmare, seceded from the rest of the committee in 1791. This split 'reflected a change in the social balance within Irish Catholicism'. The radicals on the Catholic Committee wished to break the strength of the aristocracy and they, along with the presence of United Irishmen on the committee, contributed to the increased political activity during 1791-92. The emergence of radical political ideas within the Catholic Committee also 'dealt a considerable, though not decisive, blow to the assumptions of unity, neutrality and demonstrative loyalty which had characterised Catholic behaviour in the preceding decades'.[67]

The Relief Act of 1792 was very modest in its relief for Catholics. It only affected those involved in education and law, as it dealt with entry into the legal profession. The restrictions on education abroad were also abolished.[68] Neither of these directly affected Hay's status as a Catholic. Changes on the Catholic Committee did, however, impinge on Hay. The appointment of Theobald Wolfe Tone, a radical, Protestant lawyer, as assistant secretary, was indicative of the change in the tactics of the committee, 'The change from Burke [Richard Burke was Edmund Burke's son, his appointment appealed to the deferential pro-government members of the Catholic Committee] to Tone was expressive of the change of momentum of Catholic activities during 1792.'[69] A more aggressive policy was evident among the Catholic activists. The Wexford delegates such as Devereux, Sweetman and Hay played important roles in this 'new-look' committee. Indeed, 'Wolfe Tone enthused about the respectability of the delegates elected to the Catholic Committee in 1792 from the county: "Wexford returns at last. Rent roll of their delegates, £15,000 per annum. Bravo!"'[70] Clearly,

Tone was thrilled to have such economically impressive delegates. Furthermore, commercial and political links between Dublin and Wexford no doubt facilitated the interchange of political ideas. Radical sentiment was therefore more quickly imbibed in Wexford.

Marianne Elliott has done impressive research on Tone, and she believes it was he 'who introduced Painite principles into the Catholic campaign for political rights'.[71] The ideas in Paine's *Rights of Man*, with its emphasis on an end to deference towards established authority and equality before the law, fell on fertile ground in certain parts in Ireland. With characteristic perceptiveness, Tone 'described Paine's *Rights of Man* as the "*Koran*" of Belfast'.[72] Tone was also a very efficient and energetic assistant secretary of the Catholic Committee. Anticipating the efforts of Hay, and providing him with an accessible role model, Tone helped to broaden the base of the committee. He had, like Hay, a 'ready ... pen',[73] and both men were excellent at drumming up support for the Catholics' cause. Tone, foretelling the work of Hay in the nineteenth century, 'attended Committee meetings and conducted a large correspondence but he [also] threw himself into a wide variety of useful activities, ranging from folding circulars to undertaking long journeys through Ulster and Connacht on behalf of the Committee'.[74] All this activity paved the way for the first representative election and assembly of Catholics in the late eighteenth century.

CATHOLIC CONVENTION, 1792

Ironically, the idea of a Catholic convention was mooted because of accusations made by the British government that the Catholic Committee represented nobody but themselves. One could pinpoint this convention as the moment when Hay launched himself into national politics. County meetings were held and delegates elected, and these meetings stimulated Catholic activity throughout the whole island leading up to the convention.[75] It also gave the Catholics a unity of purpose and it helped mobilise them at elite levels of society.[76] Furthermore, the 'rejuvenated Catholic Committee contributed to the visible decline in deference among the lower-class Catholics'. The 'Catholic elections to [this] extra-parliamentary convention in 1792 used the nation-wide parish structure and disseminated Painite rhetoric to a larger audience even than the United Irishmen'. These

elections, therefore, reached every parish in the country and the vital
backing of the clergy was enlisted. 'It was conducted in a glare of
publicity, through a nation-wide network of delegates and its printers
bills are a token of the outpouring of literature which so reached the
consciousness of the Catholic populace.'[77]

   Through the convention elections, Catholics were introduced
to political processes and the lower classes were also mobilised.[78]
The Catholic Committee played a crucial role in making Catholics
aware of national politics. However, not everyone approved of
the new tactics utilised by the committee. Lord Donoughmore (a
Protestant aristocrat who supported the Catholic cause) did not
appreciate the increasing assertiveness of the committee. In a letter
to his brother Francis Hely Hutchinson, Donoughmore sniffed:

> I am too proud to suffer a Catholic Junto to dictate to the people of
> Ireland and its Government, and to their own Protestant supporters
> without deigning so much as to consult them on those measures on
> which they may find their characters committed and their properties
> endangered.[79]

Grattan believed that Lord Donoughmore 'secretly hoped to conduct and manage the Catholic cause but in this he was mistaken'.[80]
As Catholic servility decreased, so Protestant suspicions increased.
Older, more cautious, Catholics also expressed their dissatisfaction
with the attitudes expressed by some of the more aggressive members of the committee. Splits between older and younger reformers
widened after the 1793 Relief Act. A physical manifestation of this
development was evident in the split between Harvey and Edward
Hay, both of whom were delegates at the convention.

   The move towards representation and the desire for a unified
and national Catholic organisation affected the Hays. The 'experience [and] … participation in group activity, in signing petitions, in
urging the Catholic case to both the Irish and, above all, the British
parliament, helped to build a sense of solidarity'.[81] Edward Hay was
appointed as one of the Wexford deputies to travel to Dublin with
the general petition to the monarch, George III. In this activity he
was closely linked with the radical James Edward Devereux, who
spent some time in France and was influenced by the ideas of the
French Revolution. Hay and Devereux were able to produce impressive support for the Catholic declaration in Wexford. Furthermore,

in local politics, Devereux, Sweetman and Hay cemented an alliance with the liberal Protestants such as Bagenal Harvey, who was later executed for his part in the 1798 Rebellion.[82] Hay, in a letter to James Gordon (a fellow historian of the 1798 Rebellion), described the election of delegates, 'Two persons deputed from each Catholic congregation in the County of Wexford assembled at Enniscorthy, on the 29th of July, 1792, where they elected delegates to represent the county in the general committee of the Catholics of Ireland.'[83] At the convention in December of 1792 there were about 284 delegates, 'All counties had returned delegates, even Kerry, where the Kenmare interest was strong.'[84] Kenmare, ironically, had seceded from the Catholic Committee in 1791.

The Catholic convention was held in Tailor's Hall, Dublin and the Wexford delegates, who were already prominent in their local areas, constituted the 'hard-liners'.[85] The liberal politician Henry Grattan, did not question the democratic nature of this convention. He wrote that it consisted of individuals from each county who were best acquainted with the views of the Catholics of Ireland. Eventually, these individuals, in expressing those views, became the spokesmen of the hitherto largely silent Catholic populace. The convention was an important confidence-booster for the Catholics, as it proved they were capable of large-scale mobilisation of public opinion, even when under attack by a hostile government. More significantly, the convention paved the way for an increasingly national Catholic Committee in the post-Union period.[86] Hay was one of the many personalities who re-emerged in the post-Union era after his introduction to national politics in 1792. He was to become one of the more persistent voices of the Catholics over the next two and a half decades. Thomas Drumgoole, Sir Thomas Esmonde, Lord Fingall, Owen O'Conor, Christopher Bellew, Lord Ffrench, John Keogh and William Coppinger were all delegates at the convention and they were in correspondence with Hay during his tenure as secretary of the Catholic Board and the Catholic Association during the 1810s.[87]

Despite the apparent unanimity of the convention, 1792 was to be a false dawn for Catholic aspirations. The strength exhibited by the Catholics signalled the beginning of the end of relief for them. Though Catholics such as Bishop Moylan of Cork and Archbishop Troy of Dublin signed the petition (to George III) at the convention, the hierarchy faced severe problems during the early 1790s.

They could not send priests to be trained at continental seminaries because of the French Revolution and its attendant turmoil for the continental Catholic Church. This predicament inevitably brought them into closer relations with Dublin Castle, as they wished to negotiate with the government in order to obtain a seminary in Ireland. They were successful in their negotiations. In 1795, a seminary was established at Maynooth, County Kildare.[88]

The Catholic Committee found it difficult to hold together different social, political and ecclesiastical strands. Divisions among committee members also contributed to the reduction in 'official' Catholic activity after 1792. For example, the 'tendency of many of the Catholic gentry to over-ride the clergy in matters where religion and politics over-lapped' was not appreciated by the hierarchy.[89] The presence of almost fifty members of the United Irishmen[90] at the 'Back-Lane parliament' (as the Catholic convention was known) frightened the older, aristocratic committee members as well as the hierarchy.

Superficially, the convention was a show of Catholic homogeneity but links with the United Irishmen and later, with militant secret societies such as the Defenders, divided the Catholic voice. For Hay, his taste for this particular kind of radical politics deprived him of his father's favour, and launched him on a career in Catholic politics which would last for three decades.

RELIEF ACT, 1793

Three major Acts were passed in 1793 and all three affected Hay's future prospects. The Catholic Relief Act of 1793 did not have a major immediate effect in Ireland, dealing mainly, like the 1792 Act, with admission to the professions. The most important provision of the Act was the granting of the franchise to the forty-shilling freeholders. Catholics were also admitted to the Bar, and 'A few Catholics were admitted to the Commission of the Peace and to serve on Grand Juries and some were commissioned to the army and the militia.'[91] The Act certainly did not satisfy the majority of the Catholic activists. 'The demand of the Catholics', Edward Sweetman, a Wexford Catholic activist, declared, 'was total. Why was Relief partial?'[92] In April 1793, the Catholic Committee was dissolved; the conservatives felt that they had achieved as much as was possible within the confines of constitutional politics. From this point on, radical Catholic activists were under pressure. Many reappeared as United Irishmen. Further reform was not forthcoming, they realised, through political agitation.

The Act did not satisfy the Catholics (including Hay), the Protestant establishment or the liberal Protestants. It managed, therefore, to antagonise many Protestants while failing to placate Catholics. Conservative Protestants felt acutely at risk, as their parliament in College Green had been sidestepped during the passage of relief legislation. John Foster, the Speaker in the House of Commons and a prominent ascendancy figure, described the crisis in Ireland thus, 'the spirit of reform will keep us for some time in a state of anxiety [and the] … late impolitic concessions have not procured content'.[93] The Relief Act, like the arrival of Earl Fitzwilliam as Lord Lieutenant in 1795, raised Catholic hopes. The expectations both events aroused ensured that the Catholics would be bitterly disappointed. Hay, like many Catholics of his generation, felt aggrieved, and the events of the early 1790s helped to propel him along the road to rebellion.[94]

Meanwhile, Pitt, the British Prime Minister, realised that in a war against France his best hope lay in courting Catholics in the short term by playing the 'Catholic card'. Irish recruits were needed to fight the French and the 1793 Act was passed partly because the British government wanted to appease Irish Catholics, who were needed as recruits.[95] The Irish parliament was not in favour of Catholic relief, as is clear from the fact that the Catholic petition of 1792 was rejected in the Irish House of Commons by 205 votes to 27.[96] While Catholics were admitted to the parliamentary franchise on similar terms as the Protestants, for people like Hay, this was worthless until the system of representation was reformed.

CONVENTION AND MILITIA ACTS

Two other acts were passed in 1793 which had a greater impact on Catholics in general, and on Hay, in particular. The Convention Act prohibited representative assemblies taking place in Ireland. This Act was a reaction to the Catholic convention of the previous year. It was designed to prevent the United Irishmen staging a similar assembly. It greatly inhibited Catholic activity in the early nineteenth century and Hay's task, as secretary, was all the more difficult since meetings had to be conducted under the guise of preparing petitions for parliament. Hay wanted the meetings to be as representative and national as possible, but the Convention Act was a constant threat to various Catholic organisations. It also discouraged further formal Catholic political activity in the 1790s, since representative bodies like the Catholic Committee could no longer meet. Furthermore, the Convention Act encouraged groups like the United Irishmen to operate in a more clandestine manner.

The Militia Act was even more significant because it sparked off the militia riots of that year. The purpose of this Act was to recruit Catholics for the militia. The demands of the British war machine, which was facing the might of revolutionary France, explain the motivation behind this Act. Hay played an active role in Wexford during the anti-militia disturbances. He was deputy governor in Wexford and attended a meeting of magistrates in July which was concerned with quelling disturbances.[97] Solomon Richards (a Wexford magistrate) later wrote that Hay was 'active and zealous as possible in endeavouring to suppress the disturbances, and to restore peace to the country'.[98] Hay believed that the riots had been caused by rumours that men were to be torn from their families and sent abroad to serve in the British army.[99] Interestingly, both Harvey and John Hay, but not Edward, signed a petition against the Act.

Reports suggested that local resistance to the Militia Act itself was widespread.[100] However, Hay believed that other factors, such as tithes, played a role in the militia disturbances. Economic upheaval in Wexford, in addition to the initial excitement and subsequent disappointment created by the Catholic convention and the 1793 Relief Act among the masses, may also have contributed to the disturbed state of the county. Significantly, Hay noted that a sectarian spirit was evident in Wexford at that time. In July 1793, the Association for the Preservation of Peace was established, and Hay was a member. He lamented that, 'at the meetings of the association, I perceived with regret an insidious spirit, eager and active to attach the entire odium of the disturbances exclusively on the Catholics',[101] and he described the prejudiced individuals as 'monsters in human form'. The dashed expectations of 1793 ultimately resulted in Catholic disillusionment, Hay observed, and this factor more than any other precipitated the riots of 1793. Finally, Ivan Nelson has argued convincingly that the Militia Riots of 1793 should be seen as the beginning of the 'suppression of the rebellion' of 1798.[102]

CATHOLIC DIVISIONS

After 1793, political stability in Wexford rapidly disappeared and this is most clearly evident in the contrasting views of older, cautious Catholics, such as the Bishop of Ferns (James Caulfield) and Harvey Hay, and the more aggressive individuals like James Edward Devereux and Edward Hay. Harvey had been active in the Catholic Committee in 1793. At a committee meeting in mid-April, he had chaired the proceedings.[103] Appointed Justice of the Peace in 1793 (the first Catholic in 200 years), he was also prominent in Wexford society. During the militia riots, Harvey was a member of the Grand Jury for Wexford and a magistrate.[104] Both Harvey and John Hay were on a committee which suggested improvements for Wexford town. In 1794, a Bill was presented to the House of Commons for the improvement of the town and harbour and for building a bridge over the River Slaney. The bridge was seen as a liberal Catholic project.[105] Hence, it was possible for Catholics of different political perspectives to co-operate. Tragically, it was this bridge which was the scene of the horrific Wexford pseudo trials and massacres during 1798.

Harvey Hay did not approve of his eldest son's more radical activities and he refused to sponsor Edward's actions. James Edward Devereux, according to the historian R.R. Madden, supplied Hay with the means to attend the Catholic convention.[106] The split was also indicative of the different attitudes towards the achievement of emancipation. On a practical level, it meant that Hay's financial vulnerability would expose him to allegations of embezzlement in the 1810s.

As an influential member of Wexford society, Harvey Hay did not want to jeopardise his standing by being tainted with 'subversive' activities. Cautious fathers like Harvey remained aloof from their radical sons.[107] James Edward Devereux and Edward Hay brought Catholic grievances onto the national and local stage in an aggressive and public manner.[108] This approach did not appeal to conservatives like Harvey who associated with the senior clergy and the hierarchy. Caulfield wrote to Archbishop Troy in 1792 complaining about the radicalism of Devereux who, he fulminated, 'acquired an amazing influence on the people by his harangues and specious promises of a total emancipation'. Caulfield was concerned that 'the spirit of this town [Wexford] ... is violent beyond belief and a general sullenness pervades'.[109] With the increasing impatience of the younger

Catholics, the splits among the two groups widened, and these divisions polarised conservative and radical groups.

After 1793, parliaments in Dublin and London were unwilling to introduce any further concessions to the Catholics. The avenues for relief closed and Catholic loyalty weakened. All this helped the United Irishmen, whose alliance with the Defenders transformed both organisations. In time, the Defenders became much more politically aware (their roots in the sectarian atmosphere of Armagh undoubtedly played a part here). Moreover, sectarianism, as well as the millenarian ideology, which fired some of their aspirations, has been documented.[110] They proved to be 'remarkably adept at fusing local grievances with an anti-Protestant, anti-English, anti-state ideology and this plasticity explains [their] … spread, and acceptance, beyond the borders of Armagh'.[111] The Defenders would find fertile soil for their ideas in Wexford. The link between the Defenders and the United Irishmen was a reflection of the need of the latter group for an army. The United Irishmen were not seen as a major threat until 1796, when a French fleet (convinced by Tone in Paris that Ireland was ready for rebellion) failed to land at Bantry Bay in County Cork. The 1796 Insurrection Act, and other draconian measures introduced by the government, worsened tensions in Ireland.

Meanwhile in Wexford, Hay alleged that he was concerned about the spread of political societies. He was invited to join a 'political society' but he allegedly declined because he did not want to get involved in politics.[112] This is hardly credible given his public profile by the mid-1790s.[113] His prominence increased when he attempted to conduct a sectarian audit of the Irish population.

HAY AND CENSUS TAKING

Hay's professed desire not to get involved in politics was no bar to his determination to establish the numerical superiority of Catholics. They were aware of their numerical strength and this knowledge was heightened by their inferiority before the law. Hay enthusiastically planned a strategy for collecting denominational data in order to provide a valid reason for immediate Catholic emancipation. He wrote to the Roman Catholic bishops, enclosing ruled paper so that each denomination could be carefully enumerated, and he asked for their help in the compilation of the statistical data. In later years, as secretary to the Catholics, Hay also sent ruled paper to the clergy whenever he wanted signatures for Catholic petitions to parliament. Hay expressed his desire to enlist the help of 'so learned a Body' who had an 'influence' on 'every liberal person'. However, Archbishop Troy was clearly nervous about the entire project. He explained to socio-economic historian Edward Wakefield that Hay's censuses 'excited uneasiness in the minds of ascendancy and Orange partisans who presented them as records of Catholic numbers to threaten the smaller number of Protestants'.[114] Clearly Hay was indulging in demographic sabre rattling. Furthermore, Hay claimed that the Royal Irish Academy (who made him a member in November 1795, because of his census efforts) was 'preparing to solicit the assistance of the Protestant clergy'. The plan, he alleged, was 'approved by Dr Troy who was willing to accept completed 'census forms'. Hay hoped that 'if his … directions [were] … minutely attended to then he would be able to produce the most exact account that ever has been given of the population of any country'.

Revealingly, Hay wanted his 'name to be mentioned as little as possible lest it might in the smallest degree retard the execution of the plan'. He also sought a list of Protestant signatures, if possible, as his census was intended to numerate all religious denominations in the country. In a model form produced in his letter to the bishops, Hay asked for the gender, profession and religion (Protestant/Catholic/Presbyterian/Quaker) of the individuals who were to be enumerated.[115]

The authorities were angry at Hay's idea. Lord Lieutenant Camden noted that:

> JW [the well-informed spy Leonard McNally] saw two letters, one from Lord *Fitzwilliam* himself and another from Burke to Hays, [*sic*] the Wexford delegate, to encourage the undertaking and to desire him to hasten it previous to the meeting of parliament.[116]

In December at Dublin Castle, Edward Cooke, the Under Secretary, claimed that Mr Hay 'is not considered highly in the County of Wexford, if I can believe Lord Ely – he is forward and busy'.[117] Dublin Castle argued that Hay was too aggressive in his pursuit of statistical data for a project that would ultimately prove to be very embarrassing for the minority Protestant elite. Furthermore, 'Irish Protestant anxiety was especially fuelled by their knowledge that they were far outnumbered by Irish Catholics, and that this statistical imbalance was not likely to change.'[118] Catholic numerical strength worried loyalists like Richard Musgrave, who declared that, 'in a menacing tone, the Papists have told us for some years "we are 3 to 1"'.[119] Indeed, a map published by the Catholic activist and antiquarian Charles O'Conor was subjected to sectarian scrutiny. This map emphasised the potential strength of the Catholics.[120] Hay was happy to play politics with the numbers game, as were other activists.

Hay received the 'approbation' of Edmund Burke for his census taking and he claimed that lay Catholics 'relished the idea of reviving the Committee'.[121] The Catholic Committee was inactive since 1793 and Catholic activists like Hay sought the support of Catholic sympathisers such as Burke in order to further their cause. Hay enjoyed corresponding with significant politicians on the subject of Catholic emancipation, and his energetic pursuit of influence brought him into contact with major British political figures such as Fox, Bedford and Ponsonby.

Though it is generally believed that Hay's census plans originated in 1795, in later years he wrote that these plans were first laid before the Catholic Committee when he was appointed a delegate in 1792.[122] In a letter to Cardinal Litta, the Prefect of Propaganda in Rome, in August 1817, Hay claimed that in 1791, he 'took an exact account of the population of several parishes in my neighbourhood, in the County of Wexford'. Significantly, he believed that 'the returns made at the time by all the Protestant clergymen in the neighbourhood, who were constant guests at my father's house' were not accurate, and that his figures 'exceeded their computations, both in total and comparative numbers of the different religious persuasions'. Hay concluded that an exact enumeration would vastly enhance the country. In fact, he meant that a census would enhance the Catholic cause. He emphasised that his census received official sanction from the Lord Lieutenant Fitzwilliam. After Fitzwilliam's recall in 1795, Hay continued with his census and 'procured vastly more returns to ground an estimation of the population, than Mr Bushe[123] [a well-known census taker] had from official sources in 1788'.

According to Hay, Ireland's population was underestimated at 5.5 million in 1803. He claimed that he 'was indefatigable and incessant in my inquiries after which I produced a conviction that Ireland contained more than 7 millions of inhabitants'. This figure is an exaggeration. It therefore questions Hay's accuracy.

Bushe calculated that the population of Ireland was 4,389,000.[124] Furthermore, Hay boasted that political economists gave him 'great credit' for his 'zeal and research'. Finally, he exulted that he could 'justly claim precedence in being the first to form a just estimate of the Irish population approaching to reality, years before any other person, which now proves undeniable from the late returns of the Population of Ireland'. Hay asked how could the 'wants of a nation be properly supplied if the extent of its population be not properly known?'[125] Census taking was very popular in the late eighteenth and early nineteenth centuries and Hay was obviously aware of the work of other demographers. He also claimed that Thomas Newenham, who wrote a demographic history of Ireland in 1805, received 'every information' that Hay 'could afford him', yet he never acknowledged Hay's help.[126] Hay's census was politically motivated since it sought to emphasise the neglect of the vast majority of the population. Hay questioned how the 'redundancy of one nation be applied to the benefit of another?'[127]

Hay was not satisfied with simply pursuing clerical support for the project. He asked the United Irishman Luke Teeling for his help, since Teeling's 'influence in the north' was well known. The sectarian mathematics of Hay's plan were obvious. 'I think it will astonish everybody as I understood ... that we were at least three to one in the north but ... by having the Presbyterians on our side ... the Balance in our favour is seven to one.'[128] Hay is clearly making the point that the strength of the United Irishmen would be greatly increased if Catholics were aligned with Presbyterians.

Burke told the sympathetic Dr Hussey (President of Maynooth College) that he liked Hay 'very much, he is a zealous spirited and active young man, he has one project in Hand of great extent and some difficulty but likely to be of very great use'.[129] The liberal Earl Fitzwilliam thought that the census was 'well calculated' and he showed it to Burke, who thought 'very highly of its utility and practicality'.[130] But in true Burkian style, he warned that 'the alleged grievances ought to go hand in hand with the Measures of rigour and coercion used to repress and punish the excesses of an impatient disorderly or misguided multitude'.[131] Even if the census indicated gross inequalities in society (which it undoubtedly would, if extra details such as occupations were documented, as Burke suggested) then these inequalities should not encourage levelling tendencies, he argued.

Hay even claimed that he had 'gained the assistance of the Bishop of Ferns', Caulfield, which is remarkable considering that Caulfield was very suspicious of any new developments. Hay explained that he received the returns of ten parishes from two neighbouring parish priests within one week and he hoped to 'finish the County Wexford in the course of three weeks'.[132] Dublin Castle was convinced of Hay's ulterior motives and it saw the census as an attempt 'to enforce the power of numbers [on parliament] … [and] the representing [of] the Catholics as the *People* of Ireland and their present political inferiority as tyranny'.[133] This is exactly what Hay wanted to do and the authorities were relieved that his project did not extend beyond an enumeration of the inhabitants of his native parish of Killmallock. While Hay's census was a failure, it is significant in that 'it anticipated a major tactic of the later Catholic movement'.[134]

FITZWILLIAM'S RECALL

Hay's census experience proved very useful in the aftermath of the recall of the Lord Lieutenant Earl Fitzwilliam, who was popular amongst liberals. The arrival of Fitzwilliam had created great excitement, as he was in favour of relief. Hay believed that emancipation would have been achieved if Fitzwilliam was allowed to remain in Ireland. But the Lord Lieutenant's speedy efforts to push the Catholic question to the forefront frightened Dublin Castle figures like John Foster, as well as the Prime Minister, Pitt. Foster described Fitzwilliam as, 'the weakest, well meaning, good man' who demonstrated his 'folly [by] being misguided by the Catholics'.[135]

Catholic alienation increased dramatically in the aftermath of the Fitzwilliam debacle, though the institutional Catholic Church was placated with the establishment of Maynooth. Typical of the establishment voice was the view of Sir Richard Musgrave, who announced that 'there is not a man of property in this kingdom that does not at this time rejoice at Fitzwilliam's recall'. More prophetically, he believed the 'predictions of his advisors that a rebellion would take place were merely false rumours'.[136]

However, the usually paranoid Musgrave was to be fatally mistaken. Hay and his radical contemporaries were now even more antagonistic towards extreme Protestant loyalists such as Musgrave and Foster. In the short term, the conservatives had triumphed over the reformers, but a price would be paid for this result.[137]

Hay was all too aware of the effect of the episode. He told Fitzwilliam that his 'recall [had] been so fatal to peace'. In his *History*, Hay claimed that 'expectations [were] dashed [and] disappointment ensued at Fitzwilliam's departure and no healing balm was provided for the deflated Catholics'. As late as 1817, Hay lamented that the event 'dashed the cup of expectations from our lips, and our bitter disappointment is still prolonged'.[138] This may seem an exaggeration, considering Fitzwilliam had left twenty-two years earlier. However, all that Fitzwilliam represented, Catholic emancipation and the removal of anti-Catholic figures from government, were still aspirations for the Catholics in 1817.

Hay received his 'first political introduction' when he utilised his census experience in an effort to reverse the recall of Fitzwilliam.[139] As he continually boasted in later years, he collected 22,251 signatures in one week for a petition on Fitzwilliam's behalf. This impressive amount is a tribute to Hay's energy and enthusiasm, but it also indicates a high level of political awareness in Wexford. Three years prior to that, 20,000 signatures were collected for a petition of Catholic loyalty.[140] According to Kevin Whelan, Hay 'spearheaded' the Fitzwilliam campaign. A meeting of fifty-four freeholders was held in Wexford to discuss the issue.[141] In 1795, three Wexford delegates (Hay, Cornelius Grogan and Bagenal Harvey) presented a petition to George III on behalf of the Catholics.[142] Both Grogan and Harvey were to be executed in 1798. In 1795 they represented the cutting edge of Wexford radicalism. Furthermore, the deputation is indicative of the co-operation between the Protestant liberals (Harvey and Grogan) and the Catholic activists (Hay). This co-operation, with its fatal consequences, reached its zenith during the rebellion.

The entire Fitzwilliam episode ensured that Hay was a well-known figure in Wexford, and the contacts he made were put to good use in later years, when he was secretary to the Catholics. In the Wexford context, the debacle had a profound effect on an already-disrupted county. Whelan has argued that:

> … the point of no return was reached with the recall of Fitzwilliam
> in 1795 (a figure who was enormously popular in County Wexford,
> where his recall was seen as a crushing victory for the hard-line
> conservatives). The posturing of the ultra-conservative, on consti-

tutional, electoral and law and order issues, gradually pushed the
independent interested into the radical camp, as the middle ground
narrowed appreciably.[143]

After 1795, hopes for the conciliation of Catholics disappeared.

HAY AND FAMILY PROBLEMS

Political difficulties were not the only barriers Hay faced prior to
the rebellion. The differences between Edward and his father Harvey
have already been discussed. Harvey did not approve of the radical
activities of his eldest son, Edward. Moreover, Harvey was disliked by
some of the liberal elements in Wexford. John Colclough (a member
of a liberal, Protestant family) described Harvey Hay as, 'not at all a fit
man for a burgess. He wishes to be a man of great Consequence, to
which he thinks nothing contributes so much as being on the grand
jury or being taken under the arm of Lord Ely.'[144]

Edward's decision to present a petition to George III in 1795 so
incensed his father that Edward was disinherited. Financial difficulties were a constant factor in Hay's career, but, despite the family
rift, it is clear from his *History* that he stayed in Ballinkeele House
(the family home) until well after the rebellion.

Hay had allegedly decided in 1797 to go to Philadelphia in
America.[145] Solomon Richards, a captain in the Enniscorthy Cavalry
and a magistrate in County Wexford, was the administrator of the
Hay family property. Harvey Hay died in November 1796 and
Edward received some furniture from the family home. He wanted
to sell it because of his proposed emigration.[146] Apparently, he 'failed
to recover from Philip [his youngest brother who received most of
the inheritance] the small pittance which was bequeathed to him'.[147]
According to R.R. Madden, who received his information from
Brother Luke Cullen (an oral historian of the United Irishmen):

> ... some short time before the rebellion ... a difference occurred
> between Captain Philip Hay and his brother Edward, by some mis-
> understanding in the division of property as devised by their late
> father. Mr Solomon Richards was an administrator, and Mr Edward
> Fitzgerald [a first cousin of the Hays] was the particular friend and
> trustee of Mr Edward Hay.'

Indeed so acrimonious was the feeling between Captain Hay and Fitzgerald that they decided to have a sword fight. This was prevented – they had a gunfight instead and Fitzgerald was injured in the thigh.[148]

According to a pamphlet published on Philip's behalf after the rebellion, Edward showed 'a disposition to dispute the said will of Harvey Hay and having taken possession of the property thereby bequeathed' to Philip, a lawsuit was initiated.[149] Philip had been away from Wexford when Edward disputed the will and took possession of the property. When Philip returned he 'instituted proceedings against his brother. The action ended in April, 1798, in favour of Philip.'[150] According to correspondence of the Hay family, Edward's share of the patrimony consisted of chattels, livestock, etc. Unfortunately these were to be auctioned on 26 May, the day the rebellion erupted in Wexford.[151] During the rebellion, General Needham made Ballinkeele House his headquarters and much of the furniture was destroyed. Hence, Hay lost all his possessions during the turmoil. Lack of finances were to bedevil Hay for the rest of his life and his slim resources undoubtedly threw suspicion on him when the Catholic Board faced financial difficulties in the 1810s.

THE BUILD-UP TO THE REBELLION

A number of different factors played their part in precipitating the rebellion in Wexford. Political divisions, the international environment, economic conditions, the sectarian atmosphere, increasing activity on the part of secret societies, and the dynamism of the liberal and radical elements in Wexford will all be discussed in turn, since they contributed to the peculiar circumstances in Wexford prior to the revolt.

Electoral divisions in Wexford were evident to contemporaries. For example, Lady Louisa Conolly of the radical Kildare family, who was described by the historian Lecky as a good judge of the state of Ireland, believed that, in Wexford, there was 'a violent Protestant and Catholic party; consequently these engines were set to work for the purpose of rebellion'.[152] The 1797 election, in particular, was very divisive. Afterwards, the split between the conservatives and the liberals was even more apparent.[153] The pacification campaign of the moderate Mountnorris (which was an attempt to keep the county tranquil and loyal) proved to be totally fruitless, since political polarisation was firmly entrenched at this stage. Hay accompanied Mountnorris on his rounds of the churches but he was very dismissive of the magistrate's efforts. He sneered at Mountnorris, who 'affected a show of concern for their [Catholics'] interests at this critical period in mere opposition to the noble Lord [Ely], his competitor for influence'.[154]

Hay was also very critical of Wexford magistrates who, he believed, contributed in no small way to the events of the rebellion, 'The horrors perpetrated in that year 1798, were the consequence of party prejudice, generally supposed to have been urged forward from political motives to weaken the country, by setting the people by the ears.'[155] Wexford needed an 'impartial administrator' since the government of the county was 'left to ignorant, presuming, and intemperate upstarts, devoid of all qualification and endowment'. Hay concluded with the opinion that these individuals were 'pushy understrappers'[156] unsuited to policing the county.

Mutual feelings of antagonism obviously existed between Hay and the magistrates. He was accused of eavesdropping and 'skulking' about every meeting of the magistrates, which had been held prior to the rebellion. James Boyd, the high sheriff, called a meeting of the magistrates at Enniscorthy early in 1798. A hostile observer noted that Hay was:

> …[in the] Market House where the magistrates assembled, though not a magistrate himself, [and] with a loud voice and insolent language, condemned the object of the meeting and insisted that the sheriff should declare to the people, of whom a vast multitude were assembled, upon what grounds or from what secret information he thus disturbed the peace of the county and damned its peaceable and loyal inhabitants by unnecessarily convening the magistrates.[157]

Clearly, Hay was not trusted by the establishment in Wexford. The absence of any sort of co-operation between the different groups in the county contributed to the total breakdown in law and order in the summer of 1798.

Religious cleavages and the sectarian geography of Wexford also affected Hay's outlook. He was living close to the Protestant settlements in the north of the county, though his own parish of Ballymurn was a 'Catholic island', according to his own census.[158] Revealingly, south Wexford (with its sparse Protestant population), in contrast to the northern part of the county, remained relatively quiet during the rebellion. Ancient animosities (fed by seventeenth-century histories, such as John Temple's sectarian *History of the 1641 Rebellion*, which was republished in the late eighteenth century) sustained rumours about sectarian bloodbaths. The activities of certain Roman Catholic priests in Wexford (eleven were found guilty of rebellion activities) only bolstered pre-existing beliefs that Catholics wished to massacre all Protestants. Though Bishop Caulfield was a 'professed loyalist',[159] his frequent admonitions to his lower clergy and flock were often ignored because of the presence of secret societies.

The sectarian strife of the era is evident from the adverse attention bestowed in April 1798 on John Murphy, a tithe proctor, *i.e.* someone who collected the hated tithes for the established Church. He was warned that he would be 'totally … destroyed' if he did not desist from his activities. Revealingly, Edward Hay and an Edward Hay junior,[160] quite possibly his first cousin, both promised to pay £3 8s 3d to anyone who discovered or prosecuted those who posted the notice. Despite the unpopularity of tithes, Hay was not willing to allow the harassment of tithe proctors.[161]

Hay firmly believed that the Orange Order (which had been founded in Armagh in 1795 to protect Protestant interests) goaded the people into rebellion. Referring to the United Irishmen, he declared that, 'their first inducement to combine was … to resist the Orangemen'. He also maintained that the partial magistrates gave no protection to the people and the 'conduct of magistrates … forced the rising of the people in the County of Wexford'.[162] Hay cleverly quoted Gordon (an impartial Protestant minister who also wrote a history of the rebellion) to support his perspective. The government was seen as giving official sanction to the depredations of the yeomanry and the notorious North Cork Militia. The militia was described as 'the worst troops in every respect now in Europe'.[163]

Furthermore, as the Lord Lieutenant Camden observed in 1798, 'military measures are so connected with the politics of the country'.[164] Hence, military excesses were seen in a political light. Yeomanry and militia atrocities, as well as heavy-handed and oppressive security, fuelled United Irish recruitment.[165] Hay continually denied that the United Irish were active in Wexford – the validity of this denial will be tested in the assessment of his work.

These activities also have to be seen in an international light. The French revolutionary wars placed enormous pressure on the British military establishment. Hence, military leaders reacted venomously to any threat to their authority.

Economic issues were also significant in Wexford prior to 1798. The malting economy was very important in Wexford, as Thomas Powell has demonstrated.[166] Significantly, 80 per cent of the malt produced in Wexford was sent to Dublin. In 1796, subsidies on the transportation of malt were discontinued. This adversely affected many Wexford merchants, including Hay's first cousins Edward Fitzgerald of Newpark and Edward Hay of Ross, both of whom had malt houses in Wexford. The maccamore-type soil (which predominated in the east and north-east of Wexford) was very rich and it was most suited to the cultivation of malt. Hence, the area was badly hit by the decline in the malt trade. The consequences of the agricultural depression were most severe in the malt-dependent areas, and rural disturbances occurred there.[167] Furthermore, those parts most affected by the collapse in the malt trade were also heavily involved in the rebellion. For example, rebel commander John Hay, Edward's younger brother, was involved in the malting trade.

Finally, the activity of the liberal and radical elements ensured that Wexford had ready-made leaders on the eve of the rebellion. Well-known individuals such as James Edward Devereux, Cornelius Gordon and Hay were active in radical politics for ten years prior to the rebellion in Wexford. Hay was not swept into the revolt against his own will. He was a committed anti-government figure. Hay's census taking and his collection of thousands of signatures on behalf of Fitzwilliam ensured that he had contact with individuals from all over the county. Hay was so conspicuous in 1798 that, according to a contemporary yet hostile army officer, lots of quarter-pint earthenware pots had the following lines printed on them, 'Long live Grogan, Harvey and Ned Hay as long as the Slaney flow into the sea'.[168] These activists were well aware of their status as a 'dispossessed elite' and their contacts with Dublin and France helped the spread of radical sentiments. John Hay had left the French army in 1793 as a protest against the execution of Louis XVI. The lack of promotional opportunities in France, as well as John's sudden departure from the army, ensured that he was very disillusioned, like his elder brother Edward.[169]

REBELLION

Edward Hay's role in the rebellion is difficult to ascertain. Louis Cullen has identified the slaughter of prisoners by the yeomanry at Carnew on 25 May[170] as the spark which ignited the revolt. On May 26, Hay was at Edward Fitzgerald's house in Newpark (only five miles from Ballinkeele). The Magistrate Turner was allocating protection notices as security and this explains Hay's presence at Newpark. Hay continually insisted that he 'refused to accept any command' among the rebels and 'that from his rank and religion and his accidental [?] connection and relationship with some who took a lead in the Rebel Army, [he] had some influence amongst them'. Moreover, he argued that he associated with the rebels solely to preserve the 'lives of Protestant loyalists in the pursuit of which he frequently hazarded his own'. He also maintained that 'in common with Thousands of the Loyal Men of the County of Wexford [he was] intercepted in [his] attempt to Escape from the said County and subjected to the absolute power of the rebels'.[171]

The Hays were unfortunate in that Ballinkeele was situated in the cockpit of 'rebellion country'. The historian Revd Thomas Handcock believed that the rebels assembled at a chapel 'near Ballinkeele'.[172] John Hay was accused of haranguing the people and entreating them to burn Wexford town and all of its inhabitants. He was subsequently executed.[173] However, Bishop Caulfield believed that, 'Philip Hay and John too were forced into the execrable business' and he hoped Edward Fitzgerald and Hay would now see the difference between their principles and his.[174] It is revealing that Caulfield did not mention Edward Hay being dragged into the rebellion. He did not trust him.

Numerous individuals testified on behalf of Hay's conduct during the rebellion, though there were contradictory testimonials also. The Magistrate Solomon Richards wrote that Hay 'succeeded in sending the rebels away … and Hay endeavoured to save' Richards. He concluded that Hay 'was not a United Irishman'. Finally, he wrote that, 'considering the popularity of Mr Hay, and he being a Catholic, he was surprised that Hay was not forced to fight with the rebels'. Martha Richards maintained that Hay 'prevented twelve prisoners being sent to Vinegar Hill'.[175]

The uncritical R.R. Madden, quoting Thomas Cloney (a contemporary of Hay and a fellow historian of the rebellion) believed that Hay was a neutral negotiator between the rebels and the loyalists. Cloney, who was clearly sympathetic towards the rebels, described Hay as an 'unwilling spectator of actions in which he had no participation, and the witness of other deeds which he had not the power to prevent'.[176] Medical practitioner and historian Charles Dickson believed that Hay's 'presence and the influence of his name in the town of Wexford were the means of saving the lives of many of the prisoners'.[177]

Moderate Protestant voices, such as Revd Gordon, a Church of Ireland clergyman, also supported Hay. Gordon praised Hay's efforts and he was convinced that Hay had no command among the rebels and exerted himself only to save lives and property. Gordon also believed that Hay's brother John was executed because of the vendetta of Grey Thomas (a member of the North Cork Militia). Philip Hay was not convinced of his brother's innocence, 'my two ill-fated brothers were engaged in their guilty schemes [the rebellion]'. According to information supplied by the loyalist Richard Musgrave, a certain Mr Vicary maintained that his three daughters saw Hay 'mustering and haranguing a large body of rebels'. When the ladies asked Hay to release their brother (a Protestant who was placed on a prison ship), Hay told them he had no influence among the rebels though he had released a Captain Burke, who believed that 'Hay was one of the most active rebels'.[178] Stephen Lett (a sergeant in the Enniscorthy Cavalry), on the other hand, swore an oath in mid-November 1798 that Philip Hay was supposed to buy Edward's furniture, which, Lett understood, 'formed part of a settlement between them'. Hay saved Lett's life.[179]

Plowden (who was encouraged to write a history of the rebellion by Archbishop Troy of Dublin, according to the intensely anti-Catholic Lord Chancellor Redesdale) believed that Hay 'commanded an influence among the people' but he was powerless against the rebels.[180] One of the more recent historians of the rebellion, Pakenham, accepted Hay's word that Lord Kingsborough, the commander of the North Cork Militia, owed his life to Edward Hay. Hay also saved Kingsborough when the rebels threatened to kill him.[181] It is not surprising that Kingsborough was targeted by the rebels: he sought and received sexual favours from pleading females and was a strong proponent of pitch capping and flogging. Much to his ill-concealed disappointment, only two 'maidenheads' presented themselves to the lecherous Kingsborough.[182]

Loyalist commentators, particularly in *Faulkner's Dublin Journal*, Sir Richard Musgrave and George Taylor were much more sceptical of Hay's activities. The newspaper believed that 'almost every Protestant family had been massacred by the assassins' and that Hay had been executed as a rebel leader. Musgrave and Taylor were convinced that Hay was a 'committed rebel'.[183] Hay claimed that he was forced to take part in the rebellion and that partial justice and military irregularities 'goaded' the locals into rebellion.

Modern historians have argued that tensions before the 1790s and 'the possibility that military depredations and the fears that these engendered over a wide area, played a major role in provoking the rising'.[184] Hay knew, then, that his argument about being coerced into revolt would be credible. He also believed that his brother John was forced to join the rebels. There were no premeditated plans for a revolt, he argued, as 'multitudes joined the insurgents for self-preservation', while the 'Orange yeomanry inflamed the resentments of an irritated, insulted, and violated community'. The principle of retaliation, according to Hay, was the motivation for revolt.[185]

The most horrific event of the revolt, aside from the burning of 124, mainly Protestant, victims at Scullabogue, was the massacre at Wexford Bridge.[186] Hay blamed Captain Dixon (the blood-thirsty rebel captain) for the mock 'trials and the killings'. Revd Brownrigg, a local Protestant clergyman who later wrote about the rebellion, was not convinced of Hay's separation from Dixon, 'Mr Edward Hay was a parade – when it was over he mounted his horse and galloped away over the Bridge as did Captain Dixon.'[187] The rebel sympathiser and Franciscan Revd Kavanagh, like Pakenham, believed that Hay tried to thwart Dixon's bloody plan to execute the prisoners, 'Mr Hay mounted his horse, and rode off on the spur to the camp at the Three Rocks to represent the matter to the chiefs of the insurgent army'.[188]

Hay maintained that he 'became insensible' and fainted when he realised what was to occur but it was he who suggested a trial in the first place.[189] This kind of 'tribunal' was not unique. Indeed, the Wexford Bridge massacres bear a striking resemblance to the 1792 September massacres in Paris and 'comply' with the injustices meted out in revolutionary times. Dickson believed that Hay relied on hearsay for information about Wexford Bridge. Hay refers to:

> ... the decline of authority of the Committee which had been
> entrusted with the public safety and he makes it manifest

that, surrounded as they were by the uncontrollable rabble, the
Committee's functions were disrupted by the influence of Dixon
and a kindred spirit by the name of Morgan Byrne.[190]

The terminology used has clear echoes of the French Revolution,
with its references to public safety. The committee of public safety
was most associated with Robespierre and the terror in France.
Wexford experienced its own terror. While the French Revolution
exported the language of liberty, it also spread the tyranny of terror.
Moreover, the Wexford committee referred to may have been the
so-called Wexford Republic, which seemed to operate as an Urban
District Council until Wexford town was over-run by ill-disciplined rebels. There is at least one contemporary reference to the
Wexford Republic.[191]

Finally, the *Freeman's Journal* reported that Edward Hay, 'a rebel
leader', had been executed but, in fact, Hay spent weeks after the
rebellion in prison.[192] The rebellion, in Wexford at any rate, concluded when Hay surrendered to the King's troops at Wexford town.

What, then, was Hay's role during the 1790s, and more specifically,
during the rebellion? Given his prominence in Wexford politics it
is unlikely that he was unaware of the preparations of the United
Irishmen prior to 1798. Considering his non-violent activities
before the turmoil, Hay must have been genuinely appalled by the
violence he saw in Wexford. Though he was not 'dragged' into the
revolt, his name and influence placed him in the self-imposed, yet
unenviable position, of a negotiator between two opposing sides.
His insistence on the retaliatory nature of the revolt is most clearly
expressed in his *History*.

Undoubtedly, his sympathies lay with the Catholics, though he
was severe on occasion with the rebels, particularly the rebel priests.
However, this criticism of clerical involvement reflects Hay's abhor-
rence of the 'priest in politics'. He used the clergy to shift blame
from the lay rebels. Hay certainly skims over a lot of his activities in
his *History*; for example, he fails to mention that he was a member
of the eight-man directory or committee (clearly modelled on the
French example) which ran Wexford town until the rebels took
over completely. Yet, the number of individuals (on both sides) who
were willing to testify on Hay's behalf clearly indicates that he did
save lives and negotiate with the rebels.

III

WRITING HISTORY AND DEFINING THE NATION, 1799-1803

How did Hay survive 1798? A combination of powerful supporters, the determined pursuit of documentation, and the fact that he was not implicated in the bloodier events of the insurrection contrived to save Hay. He was imprisoned on 3 July 1798.[193] Initially, Hay was held in a ship named, somewhat inappropriately, the *Lovely Kitty*. The historian Gordon described the ship as follows, 'a sloop had been fitted out by the insurgents, but twice condemned as totally unfit for that service, was hauled on one side in the harbour, where she sunk within a foot of her deck and remained in that situation for a month'.[194] Hay complained that the ship was 'rat-ridden' and contained twenty-one prisoners who were primarily the 'scum of the earth'. He felt these conditions were 'offensive to a liberal mind' (*i.e.* himself) and he was even refused a bed by Wexford reactionary loyalist George Ogle. The Wexford Committee, which ran the county after the rebellion, of which Ogle was a member, 'claimed the exclusive privilege of the management of their prisoners!!!', Hay fumed. This committee maintained that Hay had petitioned for transportation but Hay believed that they used a thirteen-year-old boy (James Lett) to sign the transportation form in his name.[195] This experience undoubtedly soured Hay forever and it provided one of the motivations for writing his *History*.

Undoubtedly, vengeance was a major motivation for these activities in Wexford after the rebellion. Hay was particularly vulnerable, since his brother John had been hanged as a rebel.[196] At the same time, according to one observer the 'rebels vowed vengeance against Mr Edward Hay for aiding and assisting the late Edward Turner'.[197] Hay, then, had failed to appease either side during or after the rebellion. The sympathetic historian Revd Kavanagh, maintained that Hay's 'successful efforts to mitigate the sufferings of the royalists during the occupation of Wexford had aroused suspicion'.[198] He was detained in the 'loathsome' ship for five weeks.[199]

VINDICATION

Hay was not long obtaining testimonials attesting to his innocence. In an appendix to Gordon's *History* (the first edition was published in 1801, and a second in 1803), Hay described in great detail the conditions he was forced to endure. He was placed on the ship without any trial or inquiry. The damp condition of the ship greatly impaired his health which, he feared, 'would never be perfectly re-established'.[200]

A number of individuals praised Hay's conduct during the rebellion, as well as during his sojourn on the ship and later in Wexford Gaol. Thomas Taylor wrote that he and other prisoners 'experienced [comfort] from Mr Hay's deportment: and manner towards them' and they considered Mr Hay the 'greatest friend of the Loyalists'. They concluded that 'Mr Hay was solely actuated by principles of philanthropy'.[201] This view was reinforced by Michael Bourke, captain and paymaster in the North Cork Militia, who believed that Hay 'would do his utmost to be of service to [them, and they found Hay] particularly anxious to forward a negotiation of the prisoners' during the rebellion.[202]

During his confinement, Hay wrote petitions on his own behalf, and various individuals maintained that they owed their lives to his humanity. They also denied that Hay appeared in arms during the rebellion, and that his life was constantly in danger as he challenged the rebels. Hay wrote that he was suffering from rheumatism as a result of his confinement on the ship in Wexford harbour. His subsequent imprisonment in Wexford Gaol prevented him from transacting and settling his private affairs, which meant ruination for both his health and property. In a similar petition to the Lord Lieutenant Cornwallis, Hay wrote that he had the support of all the 'Protestant Loyalists and Military Officers who were intercepted in Wexford and who were eyewitnesses of [his] conduct'. Hay was promised protection by General Lake. However, Lake was forced to leave Wexford suddenly because of the French invasion at Killala in County Mayo, in August 1798.

Hay further documented his health problems and the 'paralytic stroke' he suffered because of his enforced stay in a 'sinking' and 'stinking' ship. Cornwallis's attitude towards those who were sucked into the 'vortex'[203] of 1798, has been described by prolific historian R.B. McDowell as one of 'measured severity'.[204] Hay benefited from Cornwallis's efforts to restore peace. While others were executed or transported based on flimsy evidence, Hay survived. Nonetheless, legal historian Niall Osborough, in a forensic analysis of the legal aspects of the rebellion, perceptively notes that, it 'is not just, as early statistics demonstrate with sombre exactitude, a deadly serious business, trial by court-martial provides the focus for an examination of legal and constitutional questions that are both of transient interest and enduring significance.' His conclusion is that the state was at its most impressive and oppressive when faced with the legal challenges of the articulate, middle-class leadership of the United Irishmen.[205] Osborough's assessment would tend to support Hay's negative views of the magistrates and the legal system in general.

Hay explained that the Wexford Committee prevailed upon William Carty (a murderer) to 'swear against him'. Hay heard this informer being briefed for his trial, which was to be held on 27 July 1799.[206] His trial went ahead. Despite these problems and a change of witnesses, Hay was acquitted. The fact that this occurred in the post-rebellion atmosphere in Wexford is quite amazing, since Hay's political activities ensured that he was a target for loyalists after the rebellion.

During the trial, Kingsborough testified to Hay's humanitarianism, and this undoubtedly helped Hay's acquaintance on a charge of high treason. The following year, Hay wrote to General Hunter with a copy of his case and he described the sectarian problems in Wexford. 'The state of the County of Wexford is in mostly much the same as the County of Armagh was in the year 1795', he elaborated.[207] The atmosphere in Wexford after the rebellion certainly did not encourage toleration or mutual understanding. Hay believed that, 'during the suspension of the Habeas Corpus Act no man could be secure from the rancour of party-spirit'.[208] John Colclough, a member of a prominent, liberal, Protestant family, wrote to his mother, Lady Catherine, that 'private spleen guides the measures' of the government.[209] Hay, therefore, must have been innocent of any direct rebel involvement in order to avoid execution or at least deportation.

Later historians have documented this loyalist backlash, which particularly affected the Hay family in various ways after the rebellion. Madden believed that the loyalists did their best to get Edward Hay hanged. They had him tried by a court martial, but they were unsuccessful, 'It was not the fault of the Protestant Ascendancy gentlemen of Wexford that all the surviving members of the Hay family were not hanged in 1798 … they did succeed however in the case of his brother John Hay.' Even worse, 'they endeavoured … with all their might and zeal, to get another brother of the Hays, Captain Philip Hay, then of the 3rd regiment of foot, hanged; but the known Loyalty of this officer was such, that even a Wexford court-martial of that time (27 July 1798) were compelled to recognise it'.[210]

Captain Hay was accused of 'treasonable practices'.[211] He was acquitted but his loyalty was questioned when he claimed, as a 'suffering loyalist', £137 14s 4d for a plate of his which was destroyed at Solomon Richards's house. He eventually received £95 (a remarkable sum for a plate) but the reinvestigation of his loyalty dragged on for four years between 1803 and 1807.[212] His accuser, the Lord Kingsborough, now the Earl of Kingston, went so far as to send a 'most false and malicious statement to his Royal Highness the Duke of York', with a view to destroying the Captain's military prospects.[213] Philip Hay eventually leased the Ballinkeele estate to the Maher family in 1807 and they bought the estate in 1825.[214]

The difficulties endured by the Hays are indicative of the vendetta mentality which was evident in Wexford after the rebellion and even affected loyal citizens like Philip Hay. John Hay's wife, Catherine and her young daughter emigrated to Canada after the rebellion, so it comes as no surprise that families like the Hays and their cousins the Fitzgeralds of Newpark 'disappeared [from Wexford at any rate] in the generation after '98'.[215]

The campaign in Wexford to rid the county of any 'suspicious or subversive elements' compelled Hay to keep quiet for the first couple of years after the rebellion. At any rate, he was very busy collecting information for his vindication which appeared as his *History*. Hay was motivated to respond to the loyalist insinuations in Wexford. However, his work was not simply a response to loyalist histories.[216] Bishop James Caulfield of Ferns believed that Hay was planning to write a lay Catholic view of the rebellion long before Musgrave's work, 'the loyalist work on the rebellion', was published.

In September 1799, Caulfield wrote to Archbishop Troy complaining about Hay. He explained:

> Edward Hay dined here twice, just before he set off for Dublin; he told
> me he would call on Doctor Troy and shew him his papers … I wished

him not to pester you, which he will literally do, if he meets you, as he does with every on [*sic*] who listens to him. He is collecting Documents, Affidavits, Materials to make out his defence, and says, he will be obliged to follow Lord Kingsbro' to England to get his Testimony; He threatens the Committee here with law for illegal imprisonment and his Brother for slander, *entre nous*, he is a delicate and dangerous man: take care.[217]

This is an interesting letter for a number of reasons. First, Caulfield was correct in suggesting that Hay would have to go to England to obtain the necessary information for his defence. This indicates that Hay was determined to justify his activities during the rebellion whatever the cost. Secondly, Hay's problems with his brother regarding the family inheritance had not been resolved. Finally, Caulfield's belief that Hay was a dangerous nuisance suggests that Hay could not be trusted. Howevet it must be remembered that Caulfield was known to be an awkward individual who was suspicious of a lot of people and very antagonistic towards those tainted by their involvement in 1798.

In November of the same year, Caulfield again expressed his dissatisfaction with Hay to Troy:

> I see E. Hay holds on with his Capers. He now wishes to build a loyal reputation on the ruins of the Friars and Clergy. I told you before to be cautious with him and if you have any confidence in Clinch [J.B. Clinch, Professor at Maynooth] give the same caution. Let not my name be mentioned … My information relative to the Friars was taken from themselves individually and collectively both now and heretofore; and they are uniform and positive: one of them saw Mr Edward Hay, that day of the Massacre [at Wexford Bridge], in the forenoon, and that by chance in the street, and without any application whatsoever … Father Colfer says, that Mr Edward Hay was at Confession with him, that morning early and when going away said 'I have an Ey[e] to the Prisoners'. This made no particular impression on Colfer, because the prisoners were threatened from day to day.[218]

Notwithstanding the fact that much of Caulfield's letter was based on ambiguous and circumstantial information, it does inadvertently hint at some of the reasons why Hay decided to write a personal vindication in the disguise of a *History*. Hay's work was produced in order to clarify and, in some instances, conceal his role in the rebellion. Caulfield was aware of Hay's plans and in his usual style he wrote, 'I fear … E. Hay will furnish the public with some matter not edifying [may] God direct him.'[219]

Hay was in England between November 1799 and February 1800. During his stay there he was accused of obtaining signatures for an anti-Union petition. He did not specify who brought these allegations against him. Subsequently, he responded to the accusations, 'My object then was to wait on persons of distinction, well acquainted with my determination, as a Catholic, not to interfere about the UNION, and I was promised their utmost interest and protection, should any sinister measure against me be attempted.'[220] Hay appears to have gone to Britain in pursuit of support for his proposed work. He used whatever contacts he may have had in Britain to market his *History*.

Hay was not directly affected by the Act of Union. The Act was a response to the radicalisation of the 1790s and the rebellion of 1798. Members of the Catholic Church were involved, however. They were aware that the orgy of chapel burning after the rebellion (Hay produced a list of the Wexford chapels burnt during and after the rebellion in his book) necessitated government support in the rebuilding of these chapels. Financial support for the clergy and a veto on episcopal appointments were also mooted in 1799 as part of the Union. Under intense pressure after the onslaught of the previous year, Troy and his colleagues agreed to accept the Union and some sort of government say in the appointment of bishops, but this veto did not resurface until 1808.

The Union did not herald a new era of emancipation for the Catholics, and one individual who would dominate Catholic politics for the next four decades was vindicated in this respect. Catholic barrister Daniel O'Connell argued vehemently against the Union. He realised Ireland would not benefit from its enactment. Since the Tory party in power at the time failed to grant emancipation, the issue was taken up by those in opposition, particularly Grenville and Fox, the most prominent of the Whigs. With the passage of the Act of Union the question of Catholic emancipation inevitably became a party issue, as Hay found to his cost when secretary to the Catholics.

FICTIONAL HISTORIES

Immediately after the Union, various interpretations of the rebellion began to appear. The first loyalist response to the rebellion was the work of an evangelical Methodist clergyman, Revd George Taylor.[221] His thesis was quickly superseded by the ultra-loyalist work of Sir Richard Musgrave.[222] Echoing the lurid tales of Sir John Temple's history of the 1641 Rebellion, this graphic account of 1798 earned Musgrave the 'accolade' of 'the loyalist' historian of the rebellion.

Interestingly, both Temple's and Musgrave's histories appeared at a time of Protestant trauma, when their position was being undermined. Charles Dickson described the work as a 'monument of remarkable, if misdirected industry' and claimed that Musgrave 'missed little of any importance which emanated from Government sources'.[223] Certainly Musgrave exploited his sources to the full and his work contains many useful maps. One map clearly indicates the settlement patterns of prominent Wexford families, including the Hays. Musgrave thought that he was doing Dublin Castle a favour by producing this work. He wrote to the Lord Lieutenant Hardwicke just before Hay's book was published, because he thought that the government should be warned about the publication. 'Sir Richard Musgrave considered it as a matter of duty to lay these facts before His Excellency', he announced.[224]

Hay responded to Musgrave's allegations that the rebellion was a 'popish plot' designed to massacre all Protestants. Hay's *History* contains a report on the dispute between the two historians. Hay sent Musgrave documents to convince him 'how erroneously' the Hay name had been introduced into Musgrave's history. In May of 1802, Hay wrote to Musgrave about the conditions he endured on the prison ship and he complained about Musgrave's 'barefaced perversion of truth'. Hay claimed that Musgrave agreed to retract what he had written about the Hays but then Musgrave avoided Hay and refused to speak to him. Hay also mentioned that Cornwallis withdrew his sanction of Musgrave's book because it revived 'dreadful animosities'. Revealingly, Musgrave had dedicated his book to the lenient Lord Lieutenant, but when Cornwallis read the massive tome, he demanded that the dedication be removed. Musgrave responded, 'Hay never produced a particle of evidence to prove that what I said of him was unfounded.' Self righteously, Hay replied that his conduct had been vindicated 'as meritorious' and that he 'was personally not disliked by the people'. Hay believed that those who protected others were 'martyrs to humanity' and he concluded his defence with the retort that 'benevolence and philanthropy [were being charged] as treasonable!'[225] It appears that Hay won this debate with Musgrave but the latter's work, despite all its flaws, was a commercial success with sales of more than 3,000 copies.[226]

Notwithstanding the differences between Musgrave and Hay, they were similar in some respects. Both were indefatigable in the pursuit of information to bolster the views expounded in their respective books. An energetic pursuit of sources and a propensity for name-dropping characterised both historians. Musgrave even asked people to fill up questionnaires about the rebellion. His style of research was less than objective. He asked his correspondents for 'any anecdotes of atrocities committed by the United Irishmen and Defenders'. He reassured them by making clear that he would not 'mention the names of any gentlemen who are so good to favour me with their assistance'.[227] Over one hundred men and women wrote to Musgrave detailing their suffering during the rebellion.[228]

Both of the books appeared while the embers of the rebellion were still hot, and their publications aroused controversy. Intriguingly, the intensely loyalist Musgrave and the rebel sympathiser Hay, as well as the prolific novelist Lady Morgan, shared the same publisher, the radical Stockdale.[229] In fact, Hay lodged with Stockdale in the spring of 1803 when his book was in the press. Hay's stay has convinced Ruán O'Donnell that this 'incriminating circumstance explains his partial engagement with the [Emmet Rebellion] conspirators'.[230] However, this is hardly compelling, since there is no other evidence that Hay had any involvement with Robert Emmet's abortive rebellion in the summer of 1803. Given Hay's aspiration that his *History* would vindicate him, it is unlikely that he would have risked such an 'engagement'.

Although Hay's work was, and is, hailed as the first Catholic response to the events of 1798, the work of Church of Ireland clergyman Revd James Gordon paved the way for Hay's book. Gordon's work appeared just after Taylor's and Musgrave's in 1801. Gordon suggested that the insurgents were goaded into rebellion and that the United Irishmen were not organised in Wexford – views that would later be reiterated by Hay. In Gordon's second edition[231] he published a letter from Edward Fitzgerald to Hay, which referred to Hay's difficulties on the prison ship. Perhaps this gaol was the *Argenta* of 1798.[232] Hay denied that he had ever petitioned for transportation. Fitzgerald went on to describe how Hay was, along with other innocent persons, a victim 'of a persecuting sanguinary party … that vile body, commonly called, "the committee"'. He also

thought that Hay was a victim of 'suborned perjury' and he hoped
Hay would get a 'redress' for his grievances.[233] Gordon also published a letter by Lord Kingsborough who described Hay as 'very
unjustly persecuted.'[234] Gordon admitted that Hay furnished him
with documents prior to the publication of the second edition.[235]
Hence, the impetus came from Hay, who used the Gordon book to
defend himself.

The errors in Gordon's book convinced Hay that 'auxiliary
documents that cannot fail to convince you that the introduction
of my name into your history' was inappropriate. Hay also hoped
that Gordon's 'professions of liberality and candour may be realised
in doing justice to my present communication'.[236] Hay was determined, therefore, that his name would be cleared, and his *History* set
out to do this in a determined fashion.

HAY'S *HISTORY*

Hay's *History of the Insurrection of the County of Wexford AD 1798*
was published in March 1803. Dublin Castle nervously stalked the
printing presses prior to its publication. Alexander Marsden, the
under secretary at Dublin Castle, moaned to the chief secretary,
William Wickham, that:

> … [it] abounds with matter which it were best was not published. I got
> the sheets as they are struck off, and I am now just considering what
> steps it will be best to take, which shall of course be well weighed by
> others also. I had rather have the printer prosecute me for trespass, than
> that we should only have the satisfaction of placing him in the pillory
> after he had distributed some hundred or thousand copies.[237]

It is not surprising that Dublin Castle politicians were willing to
break the law in order to prevent the publication. Marsden even
sought legal advice on the book.[238] Hay's *History* exposed Dublin
Castle, the administrative centre of British rule in Ireland, as corrupt.

Hay's *History* is a Catholic apologia for the events of 1798 in
Wexford and a personal vindication of the role of the author during
the rebellion. Hay concentrates on Wexford, as he knew most about
his own area. He downplays the impact of Catholic lay involvement
in the revolt, and the role of certain disaffected individuals in the

rebellion is barely touched upon. It is worth looking at these gaps in the context of earlier radical activity in Wexford.

The immersion of prominent interrelated Catholic families such as the Hays, Devereux and Fitzgeralds in Wexford politics was discussed in chapter one. These individuals were not dragged into the rebellion against their will, as Hay argued. Their radicalism was never in doubt. Rather, Hay's prominence placed him at the disposal of the rebels and the establishment, hence his negotiating role during the rebellion.

Hay maintained that his work was designed to refute earlier biased histories. He was asked by his friends (nobody was specifically mentioned) to deliver this tale and thereby counteract the 'prejudices that have, for centuries, disturbed and distracted Ireland'.[239] Hay stressed the 'earnest loyalty' of the Catholics and he railed against the 'illiberal and calumnious outcries raised against the conduct and intentions of the Catholic body'.[240] He was determined to 'counter the malevolent insinuations' of his enemies and the book was written to vindicate his honour.[241]

Hay also wanted to redress the balance that had been tilted in favour of the loyalists after Musgrave's effort. 'I write … for the information of those who have been already led astray', Hay declared.[242] Yet Hay failed to divulge all the information at his disposal, despite his declaration that he wished to rectify the gaps in earlier works. For example, Hay was at Edward Fitzgerald's house the night the rebellion erupted. Fitzgerald was arrested, yet Hay wrote very little about this significant incident. Ironically, like Musgrave, Hay was indefatigable in his pursuit of information but evidence that was contrary to his argument was either glossed over or completely ignored.

Hay also used the book as an opportunity to attack the magistrates whose repressive policies, he believed, were the spark for the uprising. He did not wish to specify individuals but 'the character of an historian obliges me to mention some', he wrote![243] In this way, Hay was able to respond to those magistrates who brought him to trial. Throughout the *History*, he blamed the 'odious prejudice of religious bigotry … where the great majority of the people … [were] an object of hatred and horror to most of the superior order' during the insurrection.[244] The adverse effect of events elsewhere was also mentioned. The 'coldest unconcern' on the part of the landlords and the sectarian events in Armagh created tensions in Wexford, argued Hay.[245]

Hay totally denied that there were any premeditated plans for rebellion in Wexford. The 'trampled populace were goaded into resistance [while] … their first inducement to combine was … to resist the Orangemen'.[246] Thus he denied that there was any United Irish activity in Wexford prior to the rebellion. This view has been countered by later scholarship.[247] Hay's book was designed to screen earlier radical, Catholic activity, so that the blame could be placed squarely on the shoulders of the magistrates, the yeomanry and the North Cork Militia, whose conduct 'forced the rising of the people in the County of Wexford',[248] He wisely quoted Gordon, who argued that the people were quiet once they were left alone. Hay also used the 'Catholic numbers' argument in his *History* to empha-sise the inherent loyalty of the Catholics who fought in Egypt and elsewhere. They were the 'bulwark' of the British Empire.[249] It is not surprising that he should specifically mention Egypt, since that is where British and Irish troops were facing the might of the Napoleonic army.

Finally, Hay argued that the Orangemen were accused of initiat-ing the violence and that the insurgents followed their example. There 'seemed to exist between the parties an emulation of enmity, as they endeavoured to out do each other in mischief', Hay con-cluded.[250] Clearly, Ireland's intimate hatreds fuelled tensions.

Hay's description of his own role is one of the most interest-ing aspects of his *History*. While one might be willing to accept his work as a negotiator during the rebellion, it is not credible that Hay was a neutral bystander prior to his involvement in the events of 1798. His self-confessed 'great popularity' and his involvement in earlier political events surely ensured that Hay was aware of the preparations of the United Irishmen prior to the revolt itself. He used the excuse that the apparent disorganisation in Wexford indi-cated 'that no pre-concerted or any digested plan of insurrection existed in the county'.[251] Those who found themselves involved in the rebellion 'wished to accommodate themselves as much as pos-sible to the exigency of the moment',[252] Hay declared. However, the one striking aspect of the rebellion in Wexford is the speed with which the insurgents achieved their early successes, thereby indicat-ing some kind of preparation.

Despite Hay's obvious sympathies for the insurgents who 'exhib-ited on all occasions amazing intrepidity', he was very critical of the violence perpetrated at Scullabogue.[253] In this instance he wrote that, 'violence and cruelty are very closely allied' and he made the point (of course) that several Catholics perished in the barn at Scullabogue.[254] Hay used the argument that since the Catholics were 'not of the privileged class [they] couldn't be generally involved with the people, on the scope of authority or oppression'. But this argument is built on very shaky foundations. Not even Hay believed that the rebels did not violate the peace in Wexford and he admitted to being robbed by them.[255]

In line with his thesis that Catholic lay involvement was minimal and loyalist oppressions 'roused the already irritated passions of the people to revenge', Hay conveniently blamed the rebel priests and shifted the blame from the lay leaders to them.[256] He also made the vindictive point that all the rebel priests met violent deaths. Obviously, a notorious rebel leader like Captain Dixon could not be glossed over, though he was used to shift blame from Hay. It was Hay who suggested a tribunal (to ascertain whether or not loyalist prisoners were guilty of attacks on Catholics) at Wexford Bridge. Dixon was blamed for the slaughter at the bridge. According to Hay, somebody asked Dixon if Hay was to be consulted at the tribunal and 'on this Dixon exclaimed "is it to consult Mr Hay, who has already deserved death for the part he has taken in stopping us for so long from taking revenge of our enemies?"'[257] This ploy by Hay very cleverly shifted the entire blame onto Dixon and it portrayed Hay in a very good light. However, since Hay suggested the tribunal, then clearly he must take some responsibility. Given the fevered atmosphere in Ireland at that time, and the desire for bloody revenge for both perceived and real attacks on Catholics, he must have known that a 'tribunal' was bound to be nothing short of a kangaroo court, where the accused could only hope for rapid injustice.

Hay also gave the rebels' point of view in his work by putting words in the mouths of individuals. For instance, he would meet those who had suffered during the revolt and they (i.e. he) would elaborate on their grievances. The author, therefore, appears to be a neutral narrator for all this information when in fact he has filtered the information so that the reader receives only one side of the story.

Hay regularly used Gordon (who was seen as an unbiased observer) to bolster certain assumptions. For example, he quoted Gordon that many were 'guilty before trial', when making the point that Catholics were immediately considered to be under suspicion by the magistrates.[258] He also pointed out that no one was punished for the loyalist spate of church burning after the rebellion. Hay concluded his work with a disapproval of the 'false representations which have been sent abroad' and he claimed to have good authority for his information. Finally, he declared that an 'impartial scrutiny [would prove that the book was] extremely moderate'.[259]

Hay, then, gave the 'Catholic' response to the rebellion and in doing so he minimised the involvement of individuals like himself who had been very active in Wexford in the 1790s. Ironically, Hay did a disservice to those who politicised and mobilised the Catholics in a manner that would be repeated (with different results) in the pursuit of Catholic emancipation. The rebellion was not a Wordsworthian 'spontaneous overflow of powerful emotion' and to argue that it was negates the impact of nearly a decade of politicisation. Hay was both a creator and a beneficiary, in the short term, of that politicisation.

MARKETING THE *HISTORY*

Hay wanted as many influential individuals as possible to have a copy of his work. He used any acquaintances he had from his activities in the 1790s to distribute his book. He sent 500 copies to London through his political mentor, Earl Fitzwilliam. Even before his work was published, he wrote to Lord Moira (a member of both the British and Irish House of Lords, as well as a vocal critic of government policy in Ireland) to announce his desire to write an account of the rebellion. Hay wanted a copy to be presented to the Prince of Wales and George III, as well as every Member of Parliament. Given the monarch's staunch anti-Catholicism, it is unlikely he appreciated the gift.

Hay also hoped that the work would remove the 'vast prejudice entertained against the inhabitants of the County of Wexford'. Two months later, Hay wrote again to Lord Moira assuring him that he had 'given no exaggerated picture' of Wexford's inhabitants.[260]

The newspapers also publicised Hay's *History*, including, surprisingly, the pro-government *Faulkner's Dublin Journal*.[261] The book was published by Stockdales, 62 Abbey Street, Dublin. The work by 'Edward Hay Esq. MRIA', declared an advertisement:

> … [is] an account of transactions preceding the event [the rebellion], its melancholy causes, progresses and dreadful consequences with an Appendix, embellished with an elegant map of the County of

Wexford. The whole work contains many material facts not related in any history of the rebellion and is not sociable to the misrepresentations ... observable in other accounts, which the author had a better opportunity of avoiding, from being himself an eye-witness of many principal occurrences.

The advertisement then referred to Hay's disagreements with Musgrave and his desire to set the record straight:

The extravagant and inconsistent conduct and writings of Sir Richard Musgrave, Bart. and his reiterated unwarranted slander against 'Edward Hay' is an imperious call for an authentic detail in refutation of the misstatements that have hitherto misled the public mind, now submitted to public opinion.[262]

A couple of weeks later, the sympathetic *Dublin Evening Post* declared that Hay's book was for sale that day at a price of 'Half-a-Guinea or ten and a half shillings' (that is fifty-two and a-half pence).[263] According to Hay, the book sold over 3,000 copies.[264] However, given that he sent 500 to Fitzwilliam, this accounted for one-sixth of total alleged sales.

Within a month of the book's publication Hay wrote to the *Dublin Evening Post* to express his indignation at Musgrave's efforts to impede the distribution of the work:

I understand that some persons in a certain county have taken the liberty to prohibit the sale of my *History of the Insurrection of the County of Wexford*. They seem to consider the LIBERTY OF THE PRESS as much under their controul [sic] as the lives and liberties of their fellow subjects some time back. I gave notice to these persons that I have advanced nothing in my *HISTORY* but what I can authenticate and they ought to be sensible that I have treated them with dignity.

Hay continued in the same vein with the claim that he had not divulged all the information as this would have antagonised people like Musgrave:

I could have proved many things which my wish to appease rather than exasperate the feelings of my countrymen induced me to suppress. These persons speak of Prosecution. They seem not to have learned where law begins and power ends. Let them consider whether it is not rather for me to seek redress by an action for impeding the sale of my Book – I have been advised to take a step and I certainly shall do so, and shall go more minutely into facts, if my present forbearance is not imitated.[265]

Hay's letter reappeared twice, just to emphasise his determination not to be prevented from expressing his views on the rebellion.[266]

Because of his determination to be heard, Hay continued with his distribution of the book outside Ireland. Earl Fitzwilliam praised Hay's 'literary labours' and Grattan complimented Hay on his 'manly and able production', as well as his 'vigour and ability'. Grattan finally declared that Hay was 'one of the very few Irish Historians who … venture[d] to deal in the commodity called truth'.[267] Morgan D'Arcy, a Wexford sympathiser, wrote that he had read the book with 'singular pleasure' and he believed it to be 'unwarped by party prejudice'. Daniel Delany (Bishop of Kildare and Leighlin) was sufficiently impressed with Hay's work that he asked Hay to furnish him 'with 70 or 80 copies' so that he could give one to each priest in his diocese.[268] As late as 1817, Hay sent a copy of his work to Cardinal Litta, the Prefect of Propaganda in Rome,[269] so he 'might peruse the Work' at his leisure. Hay immodestly wrote:

> I have vindicated my Country, and the Catholics of Ireland, from the most inveterate and calumnious assertions, in the publication of a History of the Insurrection of the County of Wexford in 1798. This work has been published upwards of fourteen years, and no-one has been found to arraign my veracity in the slightest instance [this was hardly accurate], though, in contradiction to other Histories, written for the evident purpose of exciting additional persecution, against the Roman Catholic religion and people.

Hay then continued his letter with a vindication of his conduct during the rebellion:

> From the rank and respectability of my Family, and the popularity I had previously enjoyed, I was, under the popular fury and exasperation from the vengeance of those who sought their destruction. I have to say, I have saved the lives of some who sought mine; and, throughout the horrors of a Civil War, I have been alternately selected as a mediator between the conflicting parties.

He then referred to 'many literary characters' who 'expressed their approbation' of his book. 'I have to boast the sanction of the celebrated Mr Fox, who stamped the character of conciliation on the Work, which was the principal object I had in view', Hay proclaimed. Fox, the liberal politician, for his part, wrote that the 'boldness and impartiality (as far as [he] could judge) ... afforded [him] the greatest satisfaction'.[270]

Hay's work may have been written to appease and conciliate but it managed to arouse many diverse reactions from both contemporary and later writers. Various editions of Hay's *History* were published in the nineteenth century. The most useful is the 1803 Joly copy in the National Library of Ireland. As well as containing a full appendix and a 'model census' form, there is a very interesting manuscript, inserted into the inside cover, written by an army officer who witnessed Hay's behaviour in Kilmainham Debtors' Gaol in 1822. Other 1803 copies have a map of Wexford, which, according to one geographer, was the best 'map of the county that had yet appeared' and Hay's local additions such as roads, rivers and bogs 'added a touch of regional consciousness' to it.[271] There are no textual differences between the Joly copy and the other 1803 copies. Later copies such as the 1842, 1847 and 1848 editions (the latter, no doubt, published to mark the fiftieth anniversary of the Rebellion), and the 1873 New York edition, published a complete text but their appendices were much smaller. For example, the 1848 edition did not publish the introduction by Hay which dealt with his motivation for writing the book. Moreover, the 1842 edition did not contain the 'authentic detail' of the Hay–Musgrave row which had appeared in earlier editions.[272]

Given that a total of six editions were published – 1803, 1842, 1847, 1848, 1873 and 1898 – it suggests that the work was a commercial success. It is not known who benefited from the commercial gains from these sales. Musgrave's book went through three editions in the nineteenth century (the first in 1801 and two more in 1802) but Plowden's work, which had been commissioned by Troy, was a financial disaster and it was published in the same year as Hay's book. Plowden's weighty and verbose style may not have appealed to many readers. Nonetheless, Hay's work was referred to at various stages over the following decade and a half and there is no doubt he gained national fame as a result of his literary efforts.

RESPONSES TO HAY'S *HISTORY*

In order to write a critical appraisal of contemporary views on
Hay's *History*, it is necessary to situate the works within the contexts from which they derived their ideas. Writers who commented
on Hay's work can be divided into two broad, if crude, categories:
those who agreed with Hay and those who did not. The former
group consisted of individuals like Thomas Cloney, who was sympathetic to the rebels in Wexford and was still involved in public
affairs when his *Personal Narrative* was published in 1832, six years
after Hay's death.[273]

Unsurprisingly, individuals like Cloney were not willing to
implicate themselves in the events of 1798. Cloney shared Hay's
thesis that the populace was forced to rebel and he also argued that
Musgrave's assertions were 'foul slanders'. 'Mr Hay [gave] a faithful
account of the proceedings … considering the difficulties he had to
contend with in collecting information, and the danger of taking
up his work at so early a period after the Insurrection', Cloney
explained.[274] He then referred to Hay's work on various Catholic
bodies and this is perhaps the most revealing aspect of Cloney's
comments, because Hay and Cloney were in regular contact during
the first decade and a half of the nineteenth century.[275] Cloney's
links with O'Connell were surely important and his avoidance of
sectarian controversy should be seen in the light of the achievement of emancipation in 1829 and the desire for repeal of the Act
of Union.

It was therefore unlikely that Cloney would disagree with his
former friend and confidante. Cloney also praised Hay's bravery
at Vinegar Hill. Hay, 'the able and lamented author of the history
of the Insurrection [was] … the first to brave death, if necessary,
in the service of the public'. Finally, Cloney commended Hay's
endeavours in the pursuit of information, since 'he took extraordi-
nary trouble to collect materials, and at such an early period as no
other individual would be found to vindicate the character of his
unhappy countrymen'.[276]

Another individual who praised Hay's efforts wrote a letter
which appeared in Hay's *History*. B.E. Fitzgerald (perhaps a relation of Hay's through the Fitzgeralds of Newpark) was 'glad to find
through the whole of [Hay's] … compilation, so strict an observ-
ance of facts'. He exulted:

> It is with pleasure I observe also, your adherence to truth and impar-
> tiality – free from rancorous spirit of party fabrication, which is
> the true criterion that exalts the historian above the class of party
> scribblers … I give you much credit in not retorting as you might
> for your unmerited sufferings, by not exposing the crimes of some
> respectable persons [commentators like Musgrave would beg to
> differ with this viewpoint] … your labours [will meet] … their due
> reward from an unprejudiced public …

Fitzgerald concluded by quoting Sir John Davies (the seventeenth-
century writer) who believed that Ireland remained peaceful as
long as she was 'protected and justly governed'.[277] This viewpoint
concurs with Hay's argument that if people were left in peace they
would not rebel.

This argument is echoed in the work of Revd Gordon, who
has been discussed. He accepted Hay's assertion that the United
Irishmen were not organised in Wexford. Like Hay, he believed that
'no kind of communication existed between'[278] the Catholics and
the United Irishmen. This contradicts the fact that there were, as
was noted in chapter two, several United Irishmen at the Catholic
convention in 1792.

Charles Hamilton Teeling, another contemporary of Hay and a
United Irishman, leaned heavily on Hay's work for his own *History*.
He accepted that Hay suffered for others and 'encountered much
personal risk' during the rebellion, but he was ominously, and inevitably, quiet about the role of the United Irishmen in Wexford.[279]

Criticisms of Hay's activities and his *History* by contemporaries
are a little more numerous and specific than their credulous and, in
some cases culpable, counterparts who accepted Hay at face value.
The work of Musgrave has already been analysed, and despite the
obvious partisanship of his *Memoirs*, his antennae were alert to early
developments in Ireland, such as the full extent of the spread of
the Defenders. His criticisms of Hay are what one would expect
from a loyalist and must be seen in that light. Evangelical clergyman Revd George Taylor also supported the loyalist viewpoint
and he believed that Edward and John Hay were rebel captains or
chiefs.[280] Unfortunately, Taylor does not specify why he believed
this to be true. Like Musgrave, he was immediately suspicious of
any Catholics who were prominent in the rebellion. In many ways,
Taylor was a mini-Musgrave.

Jonah Barrington, the well-known writer and barrister, whose wife was a member of the prominent Grogan family from Wexford,[281] commented on the Hay family. Barrington believed that Philip Hay saved George Ogle's sister-in-law Mary Moore. She may have been under threat as the sister of the wife of a prominent and hated hardliner.

The intimate antagonisms of Irish society were all too evident in Wexford during the rebellion. Barrington also believed that Edward Hay 'had been an active insurgent during the occupation of Wexford'.[282] This 'occupation' may be an oblique reference to the eight-man committee, already referred to, which ran Wexford town during the rebellion. Chaos reigned when the ill-disciplined rebels seized the town.

One of Hay's most dismissive critics is Miles Byrne, who was active in the rebellion despite his eighteen years.[283] There was ill feeling between Hay and the Byrnes even before the rebellion began. Hay referred to Morgan Byrne, who exhibited great 'cruelty' during the rebellion, and Hay 'thought it most prudent to humour him' since Byrne had a lot of ammunition.[284] Miles Byrne was utterly contemptuous of Hay's activities during the rebellion. Hay's 'presence at the Irish camp could have been dispensed with' and his mission to go to Kingsborough's camp was 'silly'.[285] Byrne was most unambiguous about the 'rebel viewpoint'. Quite simply, he was a forceful and articulate member of the physical force tradition in Irish historiography. Because his book was first published over sixty years after the rebellion, he was most emphatic about the strength of the United Irishmen in Wexford. Interestingly, his wife, Fanny Horner, actually transcribed the history. She did not seek to bring attention to herself, and described herself as the 'widow' of Miles Byrne. Given its uncompromising republicanism, it is not surprising that Byrne was on the reading lists of Sinn Féin members in the early twentieth century. By 1948, the republican *Wolfe Tone Annual* could cheerfully promote Byrne, but Hay was seen as a 'Castle Catholic'. This well-known insult was reserved for those who benefited from the patronage of the British state.[286] Byrne, on the other hand, benefited from the French state, since he fought for the Napoleonic regime. His background as the son of a middleman placed him beneath Hay on the social scale. This snobbery is evident in Byrne's sarcastic comments:

Honest Ed Hay, one of the Catholic aristocracy, who had his brother executed [*sic*] in Wexford as a United Irishman, and chief of insurgents,

wishes to make it appear, in his narrative, that there were very few
United Irishmen in his county, the County of Wexford, because,
the reports found at Oliver Bond's scarcely made mention of the
County of Wexford.[287]

Byrne was correct in his belief that the United Irishmen were well
organised in Wexford. He was also critical of Hay's attempts to
save Lord Kingsborough, 'Hay and some of the principal inhabitants of Wexford, had the folly to expect that because they saved
Lord Kingsborough from being put to death' they would be left in
peace. However, Hay was rescued by Kingsborough, who defended
him after the rebellion. In an illuminating aside, Byrne felt that
Kingsborough should have been tortured or killed. Finally, Byrne
lamented, 'What a misfortune for Ireland not to be able to produce
one historian who could boast, that he was neither a place hunter,
placeman or pensioner of the English government!'[288] Byrne obviously placed Hay in at least one of these categories.

Byrne clearly filled in some of the 'gaps' evident in Hay's *History*.
His emphasis on the preparations for rebellion help to explain the
early success of the rebels, and, unlike Hay, Byrne was willing to
admit that the rebels were not entirely innocent. His book was published over half a century after the rebellion and he had served in the
French army for decades. This explains his clear-cut approach. His
attitude was closest to that of physical-force republicans in the nineteenth century. Byrne had nothing to lose, whereas Hay was wary of
implicating himself, or his friends, in rebellious activities.

Likewise, the remarks of a hostile army officer who witnessed
Hay's behaviour in Kilmainham Gaol in 1822 are indicative of the
contempt he felt towards Hay. He wrote that Hay 'used to get white
with rage' when 1798 was mentioned. The army officer was also critical of 'Hay's exaggerated account of the insurrection in Wexford'.[289]
A Wexford freeholder whose work also appeared in Hay's *History* was
critical of Hay's comments on the local magistrates, 'He vilifies with
singular scurrility the most respectable gentleman of that County
[Wexford] and its magistrates not only in the aggregate, but indi-
vidually.' The fact that yeomen were seen as plunderers was 'proof of
the design with which his book was written, and of the bigotry and
disaffection which he was known to possess'. Finally, the freeholder
claimed that Hay had imbibed the 'fatal infection' of the rebellion
and he had supplied the rebels with ammunition.[290]

These writers were clearly antagonistic towards Hay and their comments must therefore be treated with care.

LATER WRITERS

Later writers give varied reactions to Hay's *History*. W.J. Fitzpatrick, prolific editor and biographer of James Warren Doyle, Bishop of Kildare and Leighlin, described Hay's *History* as a 'valuable personal narrative'.[291]

In the late nineteenth century, historians commented at length on the value or otherwise of Hay's work. P.F. Kavanagh shared Hay's view that the rebellion was a response to provocation and that the organisation of the insurgents was minimal beforehand. 'Mr Hay, who on most points is an excellent authority, seems convinced that the system of the United Irishmen had not diffused itself through the County of Wexford to the extent so confidently alarmed by Sir Richard Musgrave', Kavanagh confidently assured his readers.[292] He naturally accepted Hay's thesis because it suited his own interpretation of the rebellion. He also argued that Hay was 'at much pains to obtain accurate information' and that he was, like Cloney, an 'impartial' observer.[293] Kavanagh's almost total and uncritical reliance on Hay reached its peak in his description of the Wexford Bridge massacre, as he innocently suggested:

> Hay, who seemed the good angel of the Orangemen – while the Captain [Dixon] might be termed their evil genius – suspecting that the latter entertained sinister designs with regard to his *protégés*, resolved, if possible, to thwart him in their accomplishment …[294]

Hay's ploy to shift the blame onto the rebel captain obviously convinced Kavanagh, who was sympathetic towards the insurgents and 'common folk'.[295] Kavanagh became the nationalist voice of 1798 in 1898; hence, he ensured that Hay's influence would persist.

Philip Hore, the prolific historian of Wexford, referred briefly to Hay's work as a recommended text on the rebellion, but Gordon's work was described as 'the fairest and most reliable'.[296] Charles Dickson commented much more extensively on Hay. He described Hay as 'the leading Catholic historian of the Rebellion' and the 'most reliable as he … [wrote about] incidents of which he was an actual eye-witness.' Unfortunately Dickson failed to take into account the possibility that Hay's eyewitness accounts may not have been neutral observations. He does admit that Hay's book is 'coloured by ... predilections' and Hay 'is ominously silent about the fate of his brother John'.[297] Dickson believed that Hay's 'presence and the influence of his name in the town of Wexford were the means of saving the lives of many of the prisoners' and Hay was thus described as the 'first of the "popular" historians of the period'.[298] Finally, Dickson claimed that Hay borrowed 'extensively from Gordon' and used 'whole expressions ... without acknowledgement'.[299] In fact, Hay footnoted his references to Gordon so that his work would be more acceptable, as Gordon's work was amenable to both sides. Thomas Pakenham, like Dickson, described Hay as the 'main Catholic historian of the Rebellion'.[300] Hay's status as the first historian to advocate the 'Catholic viewpoint' is not in doubt.

Modern historians have criticised Hay's one-sided interpretation of the rebellion, in the light of recent research on the background to the revolt in Wexford. Thomas Powell described Hay as a 'Catholic apologist', who used his *History* to 'clear himself of any subsequent charges'. Powell argued:

> One of the principal aims of his *History* is to discount allegations of a specific Catholic organisation behind the rebellion. In this he had a vital personal interest but his account of events prior to the rebellion which he was in a position to know at first hand is particularly valuable ...[301]

Hay was a historian who could be used with some qualification. Jacqueline Hill has placed Hay alongside Denys Scully, since they both 'stressed the heroic endurance of the Irish as Catholics'.[302] Both Hay and Scully were to play important roles in the achievement of Catholic emancipation in the nineteenth century. Donal MacCartney has described Hay and Scully as 'somewhat timid', but insisted that they both 'argued a particular political case'. Catholic writers, he continued, 'forced on the defensive', could do no more than take up their pens in the style of Hay, 'who wanted to counteract the insinuations of others'. The tone of Hay's work is described as 'partially vindictive, and partially conciliatory'.

Hay's later activities on behalf of the Catholics indicate that his earlier writing experience held him in good stead for the trials ahead. Revenge for the events 'of the past and the need to conciliate former enemies' was evident in the early nineteenth century.[303] History writing in that era was part of the history of the revival of the Catholics. Hay was part of that resurgence.

Tom Dunne has pointed out that Hay's work (along with that of many others) is 'at odds' with recent research which 'highlighted the intense political rivalries in the country over the previous decade, sparked off especially by the emergence of a new generation of radicalised wealthy Catholics, with strong kinship networks'. Historians have also stressed 'the economic, social and regional dimensions of sectarian conflict and … the importance of a strong local United Irish organisation in the outbreak and at least the early course of the rebellion'.[304] Hay glossed over these important factors, or he attributed the presence of secret societies to the desire for self-preservation among the Catholics. Dunne maintains that Hay 'began the tradition of seeing the rebellion as an irrational explosion of popular fury, explicable only by frenzied oppression!' Individuals like Hay claimed that they were 'press-ganged by the mob' into participating in the rebellion. The myths initiated by Hay in the early nineteenth century are being exploded in the late twentieth and early twenty-first centuries.[305]

Prolific historian Ruán O'Donnell, who has examined the career of Wicklow rebel General Holt, also commented on Hay's selectivity. Hay 'felt justified in taking liberties with the truth'; as a 'nationalist historian' Hay had 'ulterior motives' when he wrote his *History*. In addition to this, 'government ignorance of United Irish organisation gave him considerable scope to misrepresent certain aspects of the insurrection in that County'.[306] Hay, then, concealed the full extent of his activities so that the Catholics could be cleared of all wilful involvement in the rebellion. As Jim Smyth has argued, the '"reluctant insurgent" school of apologia released the insurgents from responsibility and placed the blame for the Rebellion squarely with government misdeeds'. The trustworthiness of this 'school' has not survived recent analysis.[307] It must be remembered, however, that although Hay's book has been criticised for its partiality, most current writers have not suggested that Hay was a rebel. He sympathised with the rebels' cause but he was not directly involved in rebel operations. There is no impartial evidence to conclusively prove that Hay was immersed in rebel activity.

Louis Cullen, the most original contributor to 1790s historiography, bracketed Hay with Musgrave since they were both 'coy on the immediate background to events; anxious to emphasise the innocence of their own sides, [and] they necessarily had to play down the provocation to the other side'. Hay was ambiguous on the United Irishmen, while Musgrave was vague about the Orange Order.[308] To be fair to Hay, he is not as extreme in his denunciations of the Orange loyalists as Musgrave is towards the Catholic secret societies such as the Defenders. In addition, Cullen refers to Hay's reliance on Gordon 'to support his own case'. Hay's *History* is also criticised for its ambiguity about important events during the rebellion, and his account, wrote Cullen, is 'quite useless on the central question of politicisation'.[309] In fact, Hay is inaccurate and misleading about politicisation. Though Hay used Gordon, they differed in one important aspect. As noted earlier, Hay ensured that (with the exception of Dixon, who could not be ignored) lay 'Catholics scarcely emerge as leaders'.[310] Gordon, on the other hand, plays down the role of the priests and blames the lay figures. Hence, Hay is totally unreliable on the whole question of lay Catholic involvement in the rebellion and he would have known most about this.

It is understandable, if not acceptable, that Hay wanted to vindicate or screen his activities during the rebellion, as he was 'harassed by accusations which dragged on through 1799' and beyond. Citing the evidence of Brother Luke Cullen, who collected oral evidence on the United Irishmen in the 1850s, Louis Cullen pointed out that Hay 'preserved' a 'cold silence' when asked about his cousin Edward Fitzgerald.[311] Louis Cullen believes that Hay was silent about United Irish activity because 'he would have found further comment embarrassing'.[312] Cullen presciently described Hay as a United Irishman in the 'civilian sense'.[313] Drawing on Louis Cullen, prolific local historian Nicholas Furlong, in his sympathetic biography of Fr John Murphy of Boolavogue, also suggests that Hay was a 'civilian United Irishman'.[314] Hay was 'anxious not to dwell on the circumstances close to the heart of the early action on the night of the outbreak when Fitzgerald was arrested' and wished to 'put his own presence in the most favourable light'. This is only to be expected given the retaliatory atmosphere in Wexford in the aftermath of the rebellion.[315]

The obliqueness of contemporary accounts may be infuriating, but it must be seen in the context of the writer's predicament. In a study which compares French and Irish historiography, Tom Bartlett suggests that 'Catholic writers developed a picture of antebellum Wexford as a rural idyll whose bucolic calm was shattered by marauding soldiers, frantic Orangemen and ambitious, restless individuals.'[316] Hay's *History* fits this description perfectly. His picture of pre-rebellion Ireland was not unlike the pre-revolutionary France painted by La Rochejacquelin. It emphasised stability and serenity prior to the massive economic and political changes of the 1790s.

Kevin Whelan has written most extensively on Wexford and Hay in the 1790s. On the whole question of making history, he suggests that, 'the mythologising began instantly … as both sides attempted to play down their own culpability for what had occurred and to affix all blame on their enemies'.[317] Hay helped to propagate the myth that the rebellion was a spontaneous response to 'Orange' atrocities. It is clear that Wexford was ripe for rebellion long before the summer of 1798.

Hay's *History* hid the actual involvement of disaffected Catholics in the rebellion. That is not to say that his book is of no use to historians. Because of his bias towards the rebels he does respond, and provide a more palpable alternative, to the Protestant paranoia of Musgrave. For example, Hay's information on loyalist depredations has been confirmed. Hay's *History* is a useful, if sympathetic, account of the rebellion in Wexford.

After the rebellion, Catholics like Hay sought to distance themselves from the radical activities of the 1790s. The United Irishmen also wanted to screen their revolutionary programme. The significance of this 'screening' should not be underestimated. Paradoxically, Hay's thesis, that the Catholics were forced to revolt, did activists like himself a disservice.[318] By denying any pre-organised Catholic activity and by glossing over the intense politicisation of the 1790s, Hay contributed to the myth that Catholic politicisation only began with the formation of the New Catholic Association in 1823. But Hay was part of a crucial generation who gained valuable political experience in the 1790s and used that experience to propel the Catholic question to the forefront of Irish politics in the early years of the nineteenth century.

Hay's book enjoyed far greater success in the nineteenth century than Musgrave's. During this period the gradual (if partial) democratisation of politics saw the balance of power shift from Musgrave's minority to the eventually emancipated Catholic majority, which Hay so fervently enumerated and politicised.

Hay's publishing history reflects its nationalist bias. The 1842, 1847 and 1848 editions were published by James Duffy's Library of Ireland in the wave of activity surrounding the Young Irelanders.[319] The 1848 edition was published with Michael Doherty's *History of the American Revolution*. The harp on the front and back of 1847 edition clearly links Hay's history with nationalism. Harps were, as Roy Foster has pointed out, part of the 'iconography of sustained struggle which was to characterise the nationalist version' of Irish history.[320] In the wake of the Fenian rebellion, a New York edition was published in 1873. Another edition was published in 1898 to coincide with the centenary of the rebellion. One edition was published in the twentieth century.[321]

Hay's nationalistic interpretation of 1798 suited the climate of the late nineteenth century. His perspective fashioned the nineteenth-century view of political leadership which suggested that, in future, the leaders, would harness (that is, organise and control) the masses. Hay was typical of nineteenth-century leaders who sought to distance themselves from the blood bath of 1798. While Musgrave's thesis harked back to Temple's interpretation of the 1641 rebellion, Hay's perspective looked forward by providing the political justification for the national movements of the nineteenth century. Because Hay emphasised the suffering of the Catholics, his work was taken on board by nationalist writers such as Kavanagh, whose *Popular History of the Rebellion* firmly placed the rebellion in the context of Irish struggles against a foreign foe.[322]

Ultimately, then, while Musgrave's work was the more successful at the beginning of the nineteenth century, it was Hay's *History* which had the greater impact in the longer term. Sir Richard Musgrave and his loyalist friends may have claimed the military victory in 1798, but Hay and the nationalists won the propaganda war. Musgrave, as a representative of the Protestant state which dominated eighteenth-century Ireland, had to make way for Hay, the representative of the Catholic nation which dominated nineteenth-century Ireland.

IV

'MR SECRETARY HAY', 1804-1811

Between 1804 and 1811, the Catholics emerged as a political force to be reckoned with, and they regularly petitioned the British parliament for relief. Hay's involvement in Catholic bodies in the crucial period prior to emancipation coincided with the broadening of the base of the Catholic movement. Seán Ó Faoláin, one of Daniel O'Connell's many biographers, suggested that the Catholic Committee in the early years had an air of 'madeira and biscuits'. The parlour politics of this era would prove to be the prelude to the expansion of the political nation. This period saw the gradual transformation of the Committee into a nationwide organisation, the tentacles of which spread from Donegal to Waterford. Hay played a major role in this development.

In discussing the Irish Act of Union, James Kelly averred that 'the *ancien regime* world of aggregate meetings, resolutions, petitions and addresses rather than the revolutionary world of mass protests, public disorder and political intrigue' provided the appropriate context.[323] The same argument can be applied to Catholic Committee in the early years of the nineteenth century. While conversant with political chicanery, they sought to convince politicians of the necessity of their cause through petitions.

PETITIONING PARLIAMENT

The Catholics decided to petition parliament in March 1805. During the latter part of 1804, and the early months of the following year, they held meetings in Dublin.[324] The most prominent member of the Committee at this stage was James Ryan, a Dublin merchant who was to fall out with the Committee when he sought a lucrative government post in 1806. Though he was not a member of the delegation, Hay was in London with the delegates in 1805. Denys Scully, a member of the delegation who was to exert a lot of influence in Catholic circles over the next decade, gave Hay one of the first copies of the Catholic petition while Hay was staying in the Portland Hotel in London.[325] Scully also mentioned in his diary that Hay called at Lord Fingall's home and the delegates assembled there 'talked upon Catholic subjects'.[326] The presenting of petitions in parliament helped Hay to forge parliamentary and ecclesiastical contacts. While in London he met Fingall, a prominent Catholic aristocrat who was respected by the Committee, and Bishop John Milner, vicar apostolic of the Midland district and later a controversial agent for the Irish bishops during the Veto crisis.

William Pitt, the Prime Minister, was approached to present the petition, but it was Charles J. Fox (a member of the opposition) who seemed most willing to take up the Catholic cause. This was very significant for the Catholics, as their cause was now associated with the opposition. Hence, it developed into a party political issue.

British politics was very unstable in the early years of the nineteenth century. Pitt had resigned over the failure to grant emancipation after the passage of the Act of Union in 1801.[327] Furthermore, George III's mental condition became unstable at the suggestion of Catholic relief. Renewed war against France in 1803 also disrupted British politics. Pitt returned as Prime Minister with a conservative ministry in 1804 but the opposition was strong. The 1805 Catholic petition was soundly defeated in the House of Commons. Nonetheless, the views of Catholics were heard in parliament once again. Over the next two decades the majority against the Catholic petition gradually declined.

In Ireland, the new Catholic body did not produce unity among the various Catholic interest groups. It was becoming clear that there was a change in the 'power-brokers' in the Committee. Ryan and the professional classes, the 'violent and ambitious men … who, having acquired large fortunes, began to outweigh the influence of the ancient nobility and gentry of their persuasion'.[328] Hay was not a member of either group, but he was loosely associated with the merchants and the barristers. There were also two Committees representing the Catholics by 1806: the General Committee, of which Ryan was a leading member, and the Dublin Catholics, led by John Keogh, who were organised in order to present a petition of loyalty to the new Lord Lieutenant Bedford.[329] Bedford was seen as sympathetic to the Catholic cause. These two groups eventually merged after considerable wrangling over representation.[330] All this indicates that the Catholics were beset by internal conflicts in the early years of the revival of the Catholic Committee.

Hay does not appear in the minutes of the early Catholic meetings. The first reference to Hay as secretary was in March 1806.[331] However, he did not become secretary on a continuous basis until 1807, as James Bernard Clinch held the position in 1806. Hay was told that he was officially admitted to the Committee in April of that year.[332]

The most significant event in 1806, as far as the Catholics were concerned, was the formation of the 'Ministry of all the Talents' in February under Lord Grenville, with Fox as Foreign Secretary. Peter Jupp suggests that Grenville was 'committed to a policy of conciliation in Ireland'.[333] Hence, the ministry was believed to be sympathetic to the Catholics. When Bedford arrived as Lord Lieutenant, the Catholics of Dublin[334] as well as those of other counties, presented him with the by-now-customary address of loyalty.[335]

However, despite this apparent activity, the General Committee of Catholics soon ran into problems because of the activities of James Ryan. Private gatherings at his home prompted the Catholics to wonder 'whether Catholic meetings at private houses, being liable to partial selection, ought to be recognised, as fairly calculated for taking the general sense upon important concerns?'[336] Hay, in later years as secretary, continually strove for full representation of Catholic views in order to counteract accusations regarding the selective membership of earlier Committees.

The effect of the Bedford Lord Lieutenancy was similar to the Fitzwilliam episode. Catholics were excited at the prospect of change only to be disappointed shortly afterwards. The Catholic Committee faced a dilemma in that they wanted to use this opportunity to petition parliament, yet the 'Ministry of All the Talents' argued that they would be embarrassed if a Catholic petition was placed before parliament. Hay was aware of this paradox. In February 1806, he received a letter from Fox, who argued that 'the bringing forward [of] any petition from the Catholics this session will rather hurt than benefit their [the Catholics'] cause'.[337]

Moreover, the landed interest and the more conservative elements among the Catholics did not favour petitioning. Continuous wrangling over procedural matters and the advisability of petitioning constrained the Catholic Committee at this time. Social, geographical and political divisions, having already been evident in the Catholic Committee of the late eighteenth century, reappeared. The peers were still a respected group among the Catholics but it was the dynamism and aggressiveness of the professional classes that sustained the Catholic Committee. Hay tried (not always successfully) to maintain some sort of equilibrium between the different interest groups in order to ensure the smooth running of the Catholic meetings.

FALL OF THE 'MINISTRY OF THE TALENTS' AND 'NO POPERY' PARTY IN POWER

The death of Fox in September of 1806 meant that the Catholics had lost one of their, allegedly, most faithful supporters. Ultimately it was the desire to placate the increasingly vociferous Catholics that led to the downfall of the 'Talents'. The Catholics decided to petition parliament in 1807. This galvanised the Committee, since most people were in favour of a petition, including the usually conservative bishops, who agreed to petition after some initial hesitation. However in a letter to Bishop Milner, Hay alluded to the 'impolicy of urging a measure which … cannot be obtained'. Yet he had to 'go through with his duty and promises' and he agreed to send Milner the resolutions of the Catholic meeting which discussed the petition.[338] Milner strongly disapproved of petitioning and he had given Hay his characteristically forceful views on the matter in a covering letter to Troy.[339] In fact, Hay supported petitioning and used the excuse of his 'duty' as a handy scapegoat. In a letter to Bedford, Hay argued that the 'petition ought to be forwarded immediately'.[340]

Furthermore, the familiar British problem of the need for military recruits during the lengthy Napoleonic campaigns, as well as the desire of 'the Talents' to placate the Catholics, partly explains the motivations behind the Militia Bill of 1807. This Bill, if passed, would enable Catholics to hold commissions in the army. George III felt he had been tricked by 'the Talents' and the government resigned over another, related issue.

The 'no popery' election of May/June 1807 confirmed the Catholic Committee's worst fears. A strong desire not to concede to Catholic aspirations characterised the new government led by Portland. Prominent Orangemen were given influential positions in Ireland and the anti-Catholic Patrick Duigenan and William Saurin were appointed Privy Councillor and Attorney General respectively. Duigenan, a Member of Parliament for Armagh City between 1797 and 1816, made it clear in the House of Commons that Catholics were 'bad subjects and hostile to the state'.[341] The appointment of ultra Protestants to Dublin Castle positions made Hay's task as secretary all the more difficult. Hay and Bedford sustained their correspondence until 1815 (Hay sent Bedford the resolutions of Catholic meetings) and Bedford assured Hay that he agreed with the aims of the Catholic body.[342]

Hay was very busy in his first year as secretary. His main task was to call meetings and keep the public informed about Catholic activities. He also circulated policy documents and invited people to committee meetings by writing and circulating copious letters with details of forthcoming gatherings. The routine paperwork, in the beginning at least, seems to have been done solely by Hay. He was an effective organiser and his extensive minutes (one report of a Catholic meeting ran to thirty-six pages) are testament to his energy and enthusiasm. Hay's voluminous correspondence indicates he was indefatigable in drumming up support for the Catholic body.[343] Hay's letters make clear that he was a middleman between the Committee and the public, a motivator for the Catholics (he urged the Catholics to agitate as much as possible) and a crucial link between the Catholics and the Committee.

His impact on policy making is much more difficult to ascertain. Hay's name appears infrequently in the minutes of the meetings. Did he write himself out of the minutes (this is unlikely given his vanity) or did he, in fact, rarely contribute at the meetings? Given his loquacity, this is surprising. If he did have any impact on developments he may have been subtle enough to conceal all traces of that influence so that he would be perceived as neutral on contentious issues.

Throughout 1807, meetings were held about five or six times a month.[344] In one meeting Hay asked for the names of individuals who attended so that he could contact them about the forthcoming meetings. The Committee, in an effort to make themselves as representative as possible, appointed persons in the cities and towns of Ireland to organise petitions to parliament.[345] The Catholic meetings provided Hay with an opportunity to alert the Committee to the reaction of Catholics who were unable to attend the Dublin meetings. Hay's correspondents expressed hopes of 'unanimity'.[346] No doubt the meetings could be wearying. The *Dublin Evening Post* criticised the 'ephemeral Catholic orators'. On another occasion, a Mr Fallon suggested that no one should speak more than once![347] During these early years, the Catholics gradually became familiar with political processes, which stood them to good stead in the heady days of the 1820s.

COMMUNICATING WITH THE CATHOLICS

Hay's most important contribution as secretary was the information he provided to a whole range of individuals whose letters have survived and are available for analysis in the Dublin Diocesan Archives.[348] Between 1807 and 1815, Hay received over 800 letters from peers, bishops, English Catholics, MPs and individuals who were interested in the Catholic cause or simply sought a favour. Most of these letters begin with a note of thanks to Hay for his 'recent communication' or 'favour'. The letters also indicate that Hay responded to the various requests and demands. This naturally encouraged further correspondence and in this way Hay maintained communication with countless individuals who would later provide O'Connell with the necessary support for 'his' emancipation campaign.

Hay's public prominence (his name appeared under the newspaper accounts of Catholic meetings) ensured that he also received letters from complete strangers. In 1807, most of his correspondents were from Wexford. By 1810, Hay was receiving letters from all over the country and in this way he was aware of the mood of the nation. For example, in 1807, Robert Meyler (from Wexford) wanted continued news of Catholic proceedings. Owen O'Conor (a grandson of one of the founders of the first Catholic Committee) wanted to know the results of the latest Catholic meeting. On the other hand, Henrietta Parsons asked Hay to write to the Duke of Bedford about money owed to herself and her little boy.[349] Hay also communicated with his relations in Wexford in order to keep his finger on the pulse of Catholic activity in his native county. W.B. Caulfield of Levitstown, County Wexford, wrote, 'In consequence of your request, I have been endeavouring to learn the opinion of the Roman Catholic Gentlemen in this part of the country in [*sic*] the Expediency of a Petition.'[350]

The secretary also kept aristocrats like Fingall informed about Catholic affairs. Fingall thanked Hay for the 'constant communication' and he also expressed doubts about the expediency of petitioning early on in 1807.[351] Hay, therefore, was cognisant of opinions on Catholic issues because he was well known and accessible. He was often invited to breakfast with Fingall and contact with Hay was useful for the former, since the latter could be asked to co-ordinate the summoning of a meeting.[352] The correspondence between Hay and Fingall also indicates that Hay was a treasurer of sorts for the Catholic Committee. In May, Fingall sent Hay £191 in vouchers for his account.[353] Perhaps this suggests that Hay was paid for his work as secretary, though in later years he always maintained that he was not. Fingall's contribution may have been a personal contribution for Hay and the secretary may have accepted it as such, but this is unlikely. The money collected from Catholic subscriptions was used primarily to pay for newspaper advertisements and the rent of rooms.

HAY AND THE BEGINNING OF THE VETO CONTROVERSY

In his position as secretary, Hay was in contact with many bishops. Most of the letters Hay received praised the activities of the Catholic Committee and it is clear that the hierarchy supported the Committee's aspirations. More importantly, they provided the secretary with useful local contacts who were interested in the activities of the Committee. For example, Bishop McLaughlin of Raphoe informed Hay that Dr Sheil of Ballyshannon would attend the Committee meeting in February. Hay had the support of the bishop, and McLaughlin assured him that the views of the Catholics at the Dublin meeting were, 'consonant with the sentiments of the County at Large'.[354] It is not surprising that Hay contacted bishops, since their position in society ensured that they would know the appropriate individuals to contact about attendance at Catholic meetings. Furthermore, they added respectability to the Catholic movement. All credit is due to Hay for harnessing this important pressure group.

However, given the volatility of some ecclesiastics, Hay may have preferred to remain beyond their control. For example, the erratic Bishop John Milner of Wolverhampton corresponded with

Hay in order to inform himself of developments among the Irish Catholics. Milner received reports of Catholic proceedings from Hay, and the secretary was invited to stay with Milner in 1807.[355] Hay, then, was a useful sounding board for those who could not attend at the Catholic meetings.

At the beginning of 1808, Hay was not immediately elected as secretary. He was usually elected unopposed, but at a meeting on 5 January he was not appointed. There was some difference of opinion as to his appointment.[356] Nobody was willing to take on such an onerous job and so Hay recovered from this temporary setback and was elected secretary. The incident suggests that Hay was not a unanimous or popular choice as in the role. James Meyler from Wexford was delighted that Hay triumphed over his enemies and received the thanks of the Catholic body.[357] Gerard O'Brien has argued that Hay's failure was the result of a clash between the 'moderates' on the Committee led by Keogh and the more aggressive members like Hay and O'Connell who wanted to petition parliament.[358] Eventually the Committee decided they would petition parliament and it was this petition that initiated the Veto episode.

Divisions on the Catholic Committee were not the only difficulties facing Hay. During August 1808, Hay travelled to Waterford under a fictitious name. Inevitably, this ploy failed as he was well known. More significantly, the authorities decided 'not to slacken vigilance of his motions'.[359] It is not clear why Hay foolishly travelled to Wexford with an assumed name. The Dublin Castle report clearly indicates that the authorities were still wary of him and he was regularly under surveillance. They may have been all the more wary of Hay as he was injured the previous year in a duel with Major John Devereux due to a dispute during the contentious election in Wexford.[360] Hay's pugnacity and indiscretion would not serve him well when contentious issues were discussed over the next decade. Nevertheless, Hay continued with his work on the Committee and his workload increased dramatically during the Veto controversy.

It is not proposed to deal with all aspects of the suggested government Veto on episcopal appointments.[361] Hay's role during the controversy concerns us most. His desire for unity among Catholics was virtually shattered by the Veto, as some Catholics (notably the aristocrats, though not all of them, on the Committee) were willing to accept some form of government interference in episcopal elections. In addition, Hay's relations with English Catholics such as Charles Butler (former secretary to the English Catholic Committee) and Edward Jerningham (then secretary) were strained by the Veto problem because the English Catholics were more willing to accept some form of Veto than their Irish counterparts. The situation was complicated by the fact that Bishop Milner was appointed the Irish bishops' agent and was very hostile to Butler and Jerningham. Such was Milner's diplomacy that he described Butler as a 'rat' and Jerningham as an 'ape'.[362]

Hay's predicament was worsened by the fact that he was not even informed about the proposed Veto. He was in London when the Veto was outlined in the House of Commons on 25 May by George Ponsonby, who believed that the Irish bishops approved of the plan. The bishops officially repudiated the proposals in September. Milner failed to inform Hay about the Veto, though Bishops Moylan (of Cork) and Troy appeared to support it in the early stages. Once Milner realised that there was a lot of feeling against the proposal, he quickly became vehemently anti-Veto. In the meantime, Hay was at the receiving end of various complaints about both the Veto and Milner.[363] It is clear from his letters that he opposed any form of Veto, for political rather than theological reasons, but Hay still tried to prevent divisions among the different groups of Catholics.

Daniel O'Connell was resolutely anti-Veto and it could be argued that the Veto heralded the arrival of O'Connell as the dominant figure on the Irish political scene. The whole controversy also witnessed the final change in the power structure of the Catholic Committee. It was noted earlier that the professional classes began to have a greater influence on the Committee in the early 1800s. During the Veto crisis their impact increased even more, as the conservative elements left the Committee since they were more willing to accept the Veto in some form. However, this was not a binary division. Some aristocrats were pro-Veto and some members of the professional classes were anti-Veto. Fingall tried, unsuccessfully, to straddle both groups and Donoughmore and Ffrench were not supporters of the Veto.[364] Nonetheless, it is noticeable that, from 1808 onwards, O'Connell, instead of one of the peers, appeared more frequently in the chair at the meetings.

The significance of the Veto controversy in forcing the public to question the way episcopal nominations were made was not wasted on Hay. He had strong views on ecclesiastical autocracy. His poor relationship with Bishops Caulfield and Ryan (of Ferns in Wexford) encouraged Hay to favour a more democratic form of episcopal elections. A bishop could nominate his own coadjutor. Hence, bishops were nominating their own successors. Caulfield was able to nominate Ryan. The latter was very arrogant, as an article in Watty Cox's (admittedly scurrilous) *Irish Magazine* made clear. It was believed that episcopal elections were riddled with simony and nepotism.[365] This debate about the domestic nomination of bishops (which Hay favoured) dragged on until the 1820s, even after the Veto controversy died down. The fact that prominent members of the English Catholic Committee, such as Charles Butler, were members of the Cisalpine Club (which favoured a more national form of episcopal nomination with a concurrent decline in the power of bishops) further complicated matters.[366]

Hay's alleged Richerism, which was a form of Gallicanism favoured by the lower order clergy, is evident from his emphasis on episcopal elections by Dean and Chapter. They represented middle-ranking clergy. In other words, he argued that the clergy of the diocese should have some say in the election of their own bishop. This was seen as ecclesiastical home rule and it was never achieved.

Disagreements over the Veto and its alternatives were not the only problems facing Hay. Divisions between urban and rural interest groups also posed a difficulty. Denys Scully explained this obstacle in a letter to Charles Butler. Establishing a representative board was difficult, he maintained, because:

> …the different cities and counties would each claim a right of election – those elected should again agree upon a central place of meeting. Many in the countryside dislike Dublin on account of the little parties amongst the merchants and orators here, these again would object to the country, and in short the business is not likely to be soon adopted in Dublin.[367]

Hay was determined to dispel the idea that the Committee was a 'Dublin clique' with no impact on the rest of the country.

He managed to remain on good terms with all shades of opinion, bar one or two awkward individuals, during this troublesome period. He continued to receive reactions to the Committee's activities from all parts of the country. For example, he received information on the propriety of local petitions and the problems

associated with the 'Second Reformation' (when Protestant evangelicals felt that Irish Catholics were potential converts).[368] This led
to an increase in sectarian tensions.

Hay also received lists of signatures for the proposed Catholic
petition to parliament. Revd James Barrett, a parish priest in Ennis,
County Clare, wrote to Hay so that the Committee knew they had
local support for decisions taken in Dublin.[369] Hay received letters
supporting petitioning from bishops in areas as far apart as Navan,
Ballina, Newry and Galway.[370] Some of these letters contained
information on Catholic grievances and the Catholic Committee
was later to set up a 'Committee of Grievances' to examine discrimination against Catholics. The Committee was clearly politicising
all grievances in order to further their political aspirations. The
bishops also reported on Catholic meetings held in their own areas.
However, Bishop Plunkett in Navan explained that he did not want
to call a meeting in his diocese because 'some Roman Catholics are
jealous of the smallest interference of the clergy in political matters'.[371] In general, the bishops were willing to co-operate with Hay.
Bishop Bellew of Killala sent three guineas to the Committee.[372]

Not all counties were allowed to support the activities of the
Catholic Committee. Dr Ryan, coadjutor Bishop of Ferns in
Wexford, opposed the decision to hold a Catholic meeting in the
county because he was fearful of the attitude of the government.[373]
He suggested to Hay that it would be 'imprudent to hold a meeting
at that time'.[374] There were differences between Hay and Ryan on
county politics and Troy knew that each of them had their 'partisans or party'.[375] The embers of the rebellion in Wexford were
still hot. In a letter to R.B. Sheridan MP, who was supposed to
present the Wexford petition, Hay criticised the 'dictatorial' manner
of Ryan and he hoped that the bishop would keep out of tempo-
ral affairs.[376] Hay felt that unless the clergy were willing to work
towards emancipation they should not impede the progress of the
Catholic Committee. The attitude of Ryan ensured that the priests
in Wexford were not allowed to act. There was apathy, as a result,
according to Wexford man, Michael Furlong.[377]

Hay was not only the secretary to the Catholics of Ireland but,
for many individuals, he was a kind of rural politician, complete
with a large retinue of clients. Thomas Cloney asked Hay to obtain
legal advice about the assizes because Hay met lots of professional
men in his work. Philip Hay, his first cousin, wanted Hay to help

him find a job for his brother, who wanted to work in a perfume shop in St Stephen's Green in Dublin. Hay was seen as influential because, as one correspondent pointed out, he had 'many mercantile acquaintances'. Owen Sinnott of Temple Hill, Wexford begged Hay to remove his son from the Wexford Militia.[378] This was a two-way process since Hay also used his local contacts to provide him with favours he required. Arthur Baker of Waterford, for example, hoped to locate the paper Hay wanted.[379]

Hay's work throughout 1808 was appreciated by the Committee. His conduct in the 'discharge of his arduous and difficult duty' was praised. Factional disputes over procedure rather than policy still dissipated the energies of the Committee, and allegations that they represented Dublin rather than national views still had to be countered. Hay, as secretary, helped to broaden the base of the Committee by keeping in contact with interested Catholics outside the metropolis. In this way he helped to increase the representative nature of the Catholic Committee.

Despite the continuing problems among the Catholics because of the Veto, Hay's work continued apace. What did his job entail? He solicited the 'correspondence of all' in the pursuit of suggestions regarding the conduct Catholic of affairs.[380] It was usually Hay who called the meetings and on occasion there were not enough individuals to form a quorum. At one 'meeting' there was no attendance except for the secretary, who came 'all the way from Wexford' in order to meet the subcommittee, which was supposed to meet every Tuesday.[381]

Hay continued to receive reports on Catholic activities, especially from his native Wexford. Thomas Cloney wanted full instructions about organising subscriptions and calling meetings. Furthermore, he wanted to know if the Catholic body needed a treasurer in every parish.[382] Financial issues were to cause strains amongst the Catholics.

As secretary, it was Hay's job to distribute circulars requesting subscriptions for the Catholic Committee. The expenses attendant on preparing petitions and organising meetings were considerable. The Committee rented rooms at Crow Street for seventy guineas per annum. They also ordered all the Dublin papers, as well as *Cobbett's Political Register*, *The Globe* and *The Morning Chronicle* for their offices at Crow Street. Later, the publishing offices of Hugh Fitzpatrick and Hay's Lodgings at 4 Capel Street by the banks of the Liffey and at the centre of Dublin's business world became the nerve centre of the Committee.[383] In addition to these expenses, the secretary was 'empowered' to employ an attendant and clerk from time to time in order to 'carry into effect the several resolutions' of the Committee.[384] Hay was also instructed by the Committee to communicate with the 'different Counties of Ireland in whatever manner may be best calcu-lated to induce their co-operation in our proceedings'.

In 1809, the Committee established their 'Committee of Grievances' which dealt with discrimination under the following headings: clergy, peerage, commercial and manufacturing, landed interest, military and naval and the Orange system.[385] Hay then received lots of information about Catholic grievances which he communicated back to the Committee. This provided him with ammunition for challenges mounted by the Committee to the sec-tarian foundations of the British state. Furthermore, it politicised Catholic disabilities. Inevitably, Hay contacted the hierarchy while secretary and he communicated the wishes of the Committee to them. The Committee sought the co-operation of the bish-ops when they were determining the religious grievances of the Catholics.[386] Hay's access to information and his role as a quasi-public relations officer suggests that he had significant hidden power on the Committee. He was also aware of developments in other parts of the United Kingdom.

Charles Butler sent Hay a 'master plan' with instructions detail-ing how the Irish Committee might encourage pro-Catholic feeling in England.[387] The correspondence was sparked off by the Veto. The pronouncements of Milner, who detested the English Catholic Committee and made no secret of it, encouraged Jerningham and Butler to write to Hay in order to counteract the accusations of Milner. Furthermore, the English Committee realised that Irish Catholics, because of their numerical superiority and majority status in Ireland, were in a much stronger position politically and were worth courting. Hay encouraged co-operation between the two groups and he sent Jerningham the results of Irish meetings. Jerningham, in an attempt to forge links with Catholics in all parts of the United Kingdom, sent the resolutions of an Irish meeting to the Catholics of Scotland.[388]

Hay was a handy go-between for various English Catholics during the early years of the Veto. The correspondence between Hay and Butler also provides us with information on Hay's work on behalf of the Catholics and his hopes for the future. Hay firmly believed that the more the Catholic question was agitated 'the better'. Catholics should petition parliament every year. He also maintained that Catholics 'at large' had to be informed about proposals which might be pertinent. Finally Hay claimed that he stood 'well with persons on all sides of the question' both on the issue of petitions and the Veto.[389]

He therefore saw himself as a conciliating force among the Catholics. Hay's correspondence with English Catholics demonstrates his desire for a Pan Catholic League, since a united movement would strengthen the Catholics. Hay's wish for unity is evident in a letter to Jerningham where he suggests a meeting for all managers in order to foster this elusive unity.[390] Butler provided Hay with ideas on how to generate interest in Catholic emancipation. 'The press should be incessantly supplied with such articles' on Catholic activities and this information should be 'forced upon public attention', Butler declared.[391] Both committees were interested in the popularisation of the Catholic question and the extensive reports of their meetings in the press suggest that their efforts were not in vain.[392]

The cross-fertilisation of ideas between the two Committees was strained by the confusion caused by the Veto. Even though Hay remained on good terms with most of the bishops,[393] he still believed that their appointments should be more democratic. In a letter to Butler he complained about the 'absurd power' of the bishops and the 'political intrigue' that characterised episcopal elections. Hay was not the only person interested in these elections, as a number of the aristocrats wanted a say in the nomination of bishops. Donoughmore, a Protestant peer from Knocklofty in County Tipperary and a staunch supporter of Catholic emancipation, was particularly insistent on the domestic nomination of bishops. This question of the domestic nomination of bishops was to cause much friction between the Catholic Committee and the hierarchy, as the latter group clung tenaciously to its independence. Bishops did not appreciate what they saw as 'lay interference'.

Throughout 1809, Hay continued to receive letters from various individuals. Many invited Hay to dinner or requested information on Catholic affairs. One individual saw Hay as influential and respectable, and asked the secretary to speak at an assizes, while another asked him to speak to an employer on his behalf.[394] It is difficult to ascertain how Hay maintained a lifestyle that corresponded with, and could sustain, his perceived respectability and status. Some letters from relatives in Wexford suggest that he had some business (probably land) in Wexford. Edward Hay of Ross (his first cousin) wrote that it was well the secretary had money.[395] Therefore Hay must have had some income in 1809. However, this may have been a false perception created by Hay in order to impress contemporaries.

Early in 1810, the Catholic Committee decided to petition parliament, yet again, for Catholic relief. Hay sent circulars to Catholic groups throughout the country in order to make the petition as representative as possible. Scully declared that there were thirteen Catholic petitions from different parts of Ireland: Cork, Waterford, Tipperary, Kerry, Kilkenny, Limerick, Galway, Clare, Donegal, Carlow, Queen's County (Laois), Kildare and Dublin. Scully was delighted that the 'No Popery Cry' had not 'daunted or deterred the Petitioners'.[396] Wexford signatures were annexed to the petition of the General Committee of Catholics.[397]

Hay was entrusted with the Catholic Committee's petition which he took to London. On 1 February 1810, the Fifth Resolution of the English Catholics was passed at an English Catholic Committee meeting in St Alban's Tavern in London. The Fifth Resolution effectively accepted the government Veto on episcopal nominations. Simultaneously, the Irish Catholic Committee was petitioning against the Veto. Hay arrived in London the next day and the Irish Catholic Committee sent instructions to him explaining what he was to do regarding 'the management of their affairs in London'.[398] While in London, Hay stayed with Jerningham. Despite political differences between both groups, Hay remained on good terms with the English Catholics.

Writing in London to O'Connell, Hay referred to 'the propriety' of the Chapters, a reference to domestic nomination by Dean and Chapter.[399] Hay argued that the bishops would prove to be a 'bar to emancipation' since they would rather entrust nominations to the King than give a say to the 'inferior clergy ... !!!'[400] Hay wanted the bishops to co-operate in challenging the government Veto and he was confident that he was the person 'most likely to induce the bishops to act the part they should do at once'.[401] This was clearly overconfidence on the part of Hay. The situation was complicated by the fact that the Pope was kidnapped by Napoleon on 6 July of the previous year, so the British government were fearful that the nomination of bishops would be left entirely in French hands. At one stage, the Catholic Committee suggested that they should be consulted about episcopal nominations. Not surprisingly, this suggestion was rejected by the bishops.[402]

FINANCES

Hay reached the height of his popularity in 1810. His visits to London in 1808 and 1810 on behalf of the Catholic cause at his own expense, as well as his 'active and persevering zeal and application, unrelaxed energy and unabating ardour', were noted by the Catholic Committee.[403] O'Connell sent a circular in June requesting subscriptions for a gold cup in order to honour the Committee's industrious secretary.[404] Many contributions were made, but Hay never received anything.

Hay's job was virtually full-time and he maintained that the duties of his office obliged him to be in 'constant attendance' at Capel Street. The Committee appeared to be in financial difficulties at this time since they had not paid their rent at Crow Street. The finances of the body proved to be the rock on which Hay perished. A Catholic meeting report made clear that Hay had the 'discretionary power to draw upon the Bank of the Right Honourable Lord Ffrench'. This aristocrat founded a bank and the Catholic Committee had their account there. Money 'expended in consequence of different votes' taken by the Committee was to be withdrawn by Hay.[405]

More revealingly, Hay's own financial affairs did not leave him in a comfortable position. A letter from his first cousin and namesake in Ross indicates that the financial wrangles between Edward and his younger brother Philip had not been resolved. According to Edward Hay in Ross, Philip was to pay Edward by instalments and their attorneys were to meet in Dublin.[406] In light of later events it is unlikely that Hay received these instalments. His uncertain financial position made him very vulnerable when bills relating to Catholic affairs began to pile up.

In an appendix to the minutes of the 1810 Catholic meetings, there is a list of the recommendations of 'the sub-Committee'. The various suggestions indicate the high level of activity of the Committee and its secretary between 1807 and 1810. The list of recommendations was impressive. They included:

> … keeping the Irish Catholics alert and earnest about their claims, soliciting the support of MPs, collecting subscriptions, sending out circulars all over the country, organising meetings at a local level,

sending petitions, appointing deputations, establishing local committees, conciliating the Protestant mind, using the Press to good
effect, removing prejudices in Great Britain and liasing with English
Catholics.[407]

Hay was involved in all of these activities, with the possible, and
revealing, exception of 'conciliating the Protestant mind'. Energetic
Catholic agitation worried Dublin Castle to such an extent that
they decided to weaken the Committee.

Chief Secretary Pole believed that 'the whole assembly [the
Catholic Committee] seem to have assumed an air of confidence
in their strength and numbers that they have never done before'.[408]
Hay played a crucial part in raising Catholic confidence and
making Catholics aware of their numerical strength. As secretary, he
gives us an insight into the workings of the Committee. Hay's work
between 1807 and 1810 consisted of promoting the Catholic cause,
keeping the Catholic body aware of national developments, corresponding with individuals who were interested in the Catholic
cause, and finally, looking after the day-to-day running of the
Catholic Committee. Hay's activities ensured that the Committee
grew from the small group that met in James Ryan's parlour in 1805
to the 'parliament' that assembled in 1811.

Information on the actual size of the Committee has not survived but it was believed that over 500 individuals attended
aggregate meetings in Dublin. However, Catholic strength became
the Committee's Achilles' heel. The representative scale of the
Committee and the fact that Catholics now had a 'common organ'
through which they could voice their aspirations worried Dublin
Castle. The continuing saga of the Veto also helped to wreck the
Committee's hopes. Tom Bartlett has suggested that in the Veto
controversy of the 1810s, 'the Catholic nation of the early nineteenth century found its voice',[409] however, this voice would be
muted in the latter part of the decade. Over the next ten years it
seemed as if Hay's efforts would come to nothing.

V

DOING THE BUSINESS OF
THE NATION, 1812-1819

Between 1811 and 1818, the Catholic body was beset by internal divisions caused by a number of different factors. Social, ecclesiastical and political divisions had been evident earlier but these divisions were exacerbated by the particular circumstances of the 1810s. Continuing difficulties with the Veto, uncertainties regarding the political views of the Prince Regent (the future George IV), increasing vigour on the part of the authorities (especially Robert Peel, Chief Secretary between 1812 and 1818) and grave financial difficulties all dissipated the energies of successive Catholic groups. Hay, as one of the more prominent members, was in the firing line. More than most, he was at the receiving end of the frustrations which stemmed from the disillusionment with the repeated failures of the Catholic groups.

CONVENTION ACT AND THE PRINCE REGENT

The first difficulty facing Hay in 1811 was how to extend the national representation on the Catholic Committee. This was difficult to achieve without contravening the Convention Act of 1793. This Act forbade assemblies which claimed to be representative. On 1 January 1811, Hay sent a circular requesting each county to appoint ten individuals to organise a petition to parliament.[410] Five persons from each Dublin parish were also elected as managers of the petition. At a subsequent Catholic Committee meeting, Hay read the answers to his circular and he provided the Committee with a list of the managers appointed.[411] Prior to this, Hay had allegedly read a report of a subcommittee which ran to 900 pages.[412] Sometimes, his enthusiasm must have exhausted the Catholic Committee.

One of Hay's most important jobs was to keep persons outside Dublin informed about Catholic activities and to encourage them to attend the Dublin meetings if possible. The additional task of dealing with local managers brought Hay into contact with local conflicts. The differences between Hay and a Dr Meyler of Wexford make this clear. Meyler's problems with the Wexford Catholic Committee, and later with Hay, culminated in a row at 4 Capel Street (Hay's lodgings and the publishing house of Hugh Fitzpatrick, as well as the nerve centre of the Catholic Committee).[413] While Hay tried to encourage nationwide involvement in the activities of the Catholic Committee, he faced the twin problems of Dublin Castle restrictions and local rivalries spilling onto the national stage.

In mid-February 1811, William Wellesley Pole, the Chief Secretary, informed the sheriffs and magistrates to act against the Catholic Committee as the Committee had contravened the Convention Act. At the end of February, a Catholic meeting was raided, but the members stood their ground by asserting that they were not a representative body and had merely met in order to prepare petitions for parliament which was entirely legal. This was Hay's central dilemma, how to ensure that all viewpoints were represented without actually breaking the law. Initially, the problems with the Convention Act proved to be minor, but the actions of Dublin Castle did concern some of the more cautious members of the Committee. Hay's role as a facilitator of Catholic aspirations suffered a setback.

However, in an ironic way, the Convention Act also helped Catholic morale. The Catholic Committee circumvented the Convention Act by organising 'aggregate meetings', which they claimed were not representative. These meetings were used to prepare petitions and ensure that the Committee was aware of the views of Catholics. In a defiant mood after the allegations against the Catholic Committee, Hay declared that the Catholics would maintain their 'constitutional rights'.[414] As a foretaste of events to come, the most prominent individuals on the Committee, such as O'Connell and Scully, managed to avoid being arrested. As Richmond, the Lord Lieutenant, astutely observed, 'all the cunning ones have kept out of the scrape'.[415]

Developments in Irish ecclesiastical and educational life also affected Hay's work. In January 1811, Troy wrote to Hay complaining about proselytism in the Foundling Hospital in Dublin. The archbishop asked the Committee 'to devise and adopt measures to prevent a continuation' of this activity. As part of the strategic co-operation between Hay and the bishops, the latter group was willing to provide Hay with the lists of names he required for petitions. In return, the bishops asked Hay for advice and help in countering the energetic evangelicals who were attempting to convert Irish Catholics to Protestantism. Later in 1811, Bishop Young of Limerick mentioned the 'insidious exertions of Methodist Bible Societies'.[416] The Methodists were the most successful proponents of the 'Second Reformation', particularly as some of their missionaries, such as the colourful Gideon Ouseley, were able to preach in the Irish language.[417] By '1816 there were twenty missionaries working on fourteen stations dotted throughout the country.'[418] These communications on the general sectarian tensions generated by proselytism suggest that Hay was an Ombudsman for Irish Catholics. His accessibility and prominence ensured that individuals turned to Hay for help.

The biggest challenge Hay faced in 1811 was dealing with the changed political circumstances after the appointment of future George IV as Prince Regent. When George III became permanently insane, the new monarch created a lot of excitement amongst the Catholics. George III's views on Catholic emancipation were well known, but it was believed (erroneously) that the Regent was sympathetic to emancipation. Some even hoped that a change in personnel at Dublin Castle was imminent. Hence, the Catholic Committee decided to present an address of loyalty to the Regent and simultaneously they petitioned for the removal of the Viceroy, Richmond and the Chief Secretary, Pole.

In March 1811, Hay wrote to those chosen to present the address but he failed to mention the petition. They may have been in favour of presenting an address; supporting the petition was a different matter. The forty-six replies make interesting reading.[419] The majority were direct or veiled refusals, with many citing their health or the weather as reasons for their non-attendance. It can be inferred that Hay approved of the petition for the removal of Richmond and Pole since he was part of the more aggressively resolute group on the Committee whose dominance amongst the Catholics increased as the decade progressed.

The peers on the Committee did not want to antagonise the Regent. Donoughmore wrote to his brother Francis Hely Hutchinson. He had 'been in correspondence with Hay for the purpose of preventing their addressing the Prince'.[420] It is a measure of the change in the hitherto deferential stance of the Committee that Donoughmore and other aristocrats were not heeded.

The presentation of petitions in London caused other problems for Hay. The central question was one of autonomy. Were the delegates responsible to the Committee or to themselves only? This proved to be a thorny question. Hay was an intermediary between the Committee and the delegates but he was not on the delegation himself. Hay usually went to London as secretary and not as an official member of the delegation. It was decided that the secretary, 'as a gentleman could tell the peers of the general feeling of the Committee regarding the duty of the peers'.[421] As divisions between the aristocratic 'old leaders' and the professional 'new leaders' deepened, the former were less willing to take instructions from the latter. Hay's job as the communicator of the views of the Committee was therefore quite onerous and required great diplomacy.

PETITIONING PROBLEMS

Despite mixed views on the petition in 1811, Hay's countrywide circulars evoked an overwhelming response. Over 1,000 circulars and 5,000 letters were despatched throughout Ireland.[422] Hay's circular to the clergy asking for the signatures to the parliamentary petition proved to be particularly fruitful. Not surprisingly, signatures were collected after Masses.[423] In total, 15,000 signatures were collected and 5,000 alone at two Catholic chapels.[424] Clearly, Hay's census experience stood him in good stead in this regard. That is not to say that the Catholics presented a united front. In a characteristic show of independence, Cork Catholics presented their own petitions. Hay was asked not to correspond with them.[425] Dublin Castle took great delight in this apparent disunity. Richmond believed that the Catholics quarrelled 'so much as to make themselves ridiculous'.[426] Predictably, the question of the autonomy of the delegates was a matter of debate. Some members of the Committee felt that the activities of the delegates should be regulated and responsive to the wishes of the Committee, while others thought that the delegates had a *carte blanche* in London.

The arrangement of the 1811 petition to parliament and the address to the Prince Regent was confided to the care of Hay, who was instructed to go to England.[427] Obviously, those who thought that the delegates should take their instructions from the Committee had triumphed. Hay argued that the petition was 'not sufficiently courtly' but it could not be changed.[428] At a Committee meeting, it was noted that the reference to the proselytising activities of Protestants and others was seen as offensive but once the petition was submitted it could not be altered.[429] The significance of this from the point of view of Hay and the Committee should not be underestimated.

The 1812 petition, which contained insulting references to the Regent (known as the 'Witchery Resolutions'), rebounded on the delegates as well as Hay, though most of them were unaware of the existence of the offensive resolutions. The 'Witchery Resolutions' referred to comments, allegedly made at an aggregate meeting on 18 June, which blamed the Regent's so-called change of mind regarding the Catholic question on the 'baneful' influence of the Tory marchioness of Hertford.[430] To add to their travails, Donoughmore did not have a high opinion of some of the delegates, though it must be noted that he was known as a touchy individual. He complained that the delegates were only interested in advancing 'their own particular interests', while he reserved an even more damning condemnation for Hay who, he claimed, simply sought 'remuneration from his own countrymen'.[431] Donoughmore's criticisms may have stemmed from the fact that he did not approve of a petition at this time. His comments on Hay may have arisen from a resolution that the Committee was supposed to pay the expenses of the delegates. However, as later events indicate, these reimbursements were not forthcoming.

ECCLESIASTICAL AFFAIRS

The Veto question continued to have an impact on Hay's work. Like a lot of prominent Catholics, Hay wanted to play a role in the activities of the Irish Catholic Church.[432] Catholic Committee members, such as Hay and O'Connell, who were anti-Veto, were willing to manipulate ecclesiastical divisions in order to ensure that unqualified emancipation and nothing less was sought. O'Connell was willing to pit seculars (diocesan clergy) against regulars (monks and brothers). He believed that the friars would replace the Veto priests. Oliver McDonagh argued that 'the friars appear to have constituted a species of ecclesiastical left wing at this stage'.[433]

Hay complained to Jerningham about the adverse effect of combative Bishop John Milner (the Irish bishop's agent) on Anglo-Irish relations. Hay rejected Milner's interference in Irish political affairs and he believed that the bishops were 'the greatest bar to … final emancipation' because they refused to accept any form of domestic nomination of bishops. Hay also deplored the disunity among the Catholics, due, in no small part, to the pronouncements of Milner. Hay promised to communicate with Jerningham directly because of the bad feeling between the English and Irish Catholic Committees.[434]

English Catholics were more willing to accept some form of Veto than their Irish counterparts. The situation was complicated by the fact that Bishop Milner was appointed the Irish bishops' agent and was very hostile to Butler and Jerningham. As we have read, Milner's diplomacy was such that he described Butler as a 'rat' and Jerningham as an 'ape'.[435] It is an indication of Hay's impotence as a conciliating force between the two Irish and English Committees that Bishop Poynter, vicar apostolic of the London district and much detested by Milner, expressed his hope that 'mutual attachment and co-operation' would exist between the English and Irish Catholics.[436] This aspiration did not become a reality in the 1810s.

HAY'S WORK APPRECIATED

Despite the difficulties faced by Hay on ecclesiastical and political fronts, he continued to communicate with individuals in Ireland on the Catholic question and related matters. He occasionally received resolutions of local meetings, which he published.[437] Hay, then, proved to be a valuable public relations officer for the Catholics outside Dublin. When Lord Fingall went to Edinburgh because his son Lord Killeen was studying there, Hay kept him informed about events in Ireland. Fingall praised Hay's 'devotion' to the Catholic cause and his 'constant attention' to the needs of the Fingall family while they were out of the country. Likewise, Fingall kept Hay informed about events in his native County Meath and he sent Hay the resolutions of the Meath Catholics.[438]

The secretary continued to urge attendance at Catholic Committee meetings, despite the difficulties circumventing the Convention Act. In this respect, Hay was an important motivating force for the Catholics and his efforts were recognised by the Committee. In April 1811, the conduct of Hay, in refusing to destroy or deliver up certain papers, was praised. Donoughmore had written to Hay,[439] but a couple of weeks later it was questioned whether the communication was a private one to Hay or a public one for the Committee.[440] Questions about private or public communications were later to cause problems for Hay. As a prominent individual, it was often difficult to ascertain whether information passed to him was for the public domain or for his own private use.

In recognition of his services to the Catholics, the Committee awarded Hay £500. O'Connell made a very complimentary speech about Hay and he praised the secretary's 'disinterested nature' and his desire to help the Catholics 'without ever seeking or expecting any other reward than the consciousness of having benefited his country'.[441] Hay was also toasted at a 'Dinner for Friends of Toleration'.[442] There is no evidence that Hay ever actually received the money he was promised. However, there was a reference to the money and his 'invaluable' contribution to the Catholic cause several months later.[443] Repeatedly, resolutions passed endeavouring to reward the services of Hay. After his death, it transpired that Hay had never received any monetary rewards from the Catholic Committee.

In September 1811, Hay attended a Wexford Catholic meeting.[444] When he returned to Dublin he wrote to O'Connell, 'I have endeavoured to bring the principal Catholics here together to consult on what is best to be done on the 19th when the Committee are [sic] meet.'[445] But the Committee still had difficulties because of the Convention Act and in December a meeting was dispersed. The Committee decided to be renamed the Catholic Board and hold aggregate meetings, that is, public instead of general meetings, in order to avoid prosecution under the Act. Despite these superficial changes, the basic functions of the Committee remained the same. At a meeting on St Stephen's Day, 450 gentlemen were appointed to prepare a petition. Outside the meeting 2,000 people awaited the result of the Board's deliberations.[446] On the eve of 1812, then, the future looked bright for Hay. He was a prominent and popular figure among Catholics and his efforts to encourage as many people as possible to pursue the cause of Catholic emancipation were beginning to bear fruit.

THE 'WITCHERY RESOLUTIONS' AND FINANCIAL PROBLEMS

Catholic enthusiasms for the Prince Regent waned in 1812, when it became apparent that he was not going to facilitate the

Catholics. This realisation, in turn, led to the devastating 'Witchery Resolutions' and these resolutions, along with the continued imposition of the Convention Act as well as financial problems, made 1812 a very trying year for Hay.

In February, Hay refused to summon the Board 'unless he could be satisfied by the opinion of some of the first law officers at the bar that it was not a body so constituted as to come within prohibition of the Convention Act'. Hay concurred 'with Fingall and consequently refused to summon the Board'. Meanwhile, O'Connell, Scully and Dr Dromgoole (who occasionally acted as secretary for the Catholics) dissented with Hay and Fingall.

The power brokers on the Board – O'Connell, Scully and Dromgoole – called a meeting for 22 March. According to the report, which made its way to Dublin Castle, there were 'various feelings and opinions' at the meeting.[447] Clearly there were rifts amongst the more dynamic Catholics. Hay was usually associated with the more aggressive elements on the Board, such as O'Connell and Scully. However, his friendship with Fingall and his earlier acrimonious experiences with the authorities in Wexford encouraged him to be more reticent. This is the first instance of a difference of opinion between O'Connell and Hay. Up to this point, Hay was one of O'Connell's greatest supporters. From now on relations between the two would deteriorate.

The 'Witchery Resolutions' were reputed to have emanated from Scully and Lord Donoughmore. The latter, in a speech on the Irish Catholic petition, referred to 'the allurements of Calypso's court [and] the charms of that matured enchantress'. This alleged enchantress, Lady Hertford (a Tory supporter), was accused of gaining 'possession of the royal ear'.[448] Hay had nothing to do with these resolutions. In later years he was annoyed that they should have been introduced in a Machiavellian fashion by Scully, without the agreement of the Board. The resolutions, Hay claimed, were not representative of the views of the Catholics and they were an insult to 'a Lady of the highest rank'.[449] More significantly, Hay believed that these resolutions antagonised many of the Catholic Board's parliamentary friends. In a letter to the Dublin-published *Carrick Morning Post*, Hay described his efforts on behalf of the Catholics. He explained that, during the course of his work, he was 'fortunate in cultivating and increasing [parliamentary] … acquaintances from time to time while engaged in London in the presentation of Catholic Addresses'. This may have been an exaggeration, since Hay liked to see himself as a major player in Anglo-Irish politics. Admittedly, he was in correspondence with the Duke of York and various British aristocrats and politicians.[450] His embarrassment must have been acute when he heard about events at the Catholic meeting and his relations with his 'parliamentary acquaintances' were undoubtedly strained by these events. Hay was in London with the Catholic petition when the resolutions were passed and he believed that they would never have been passed had he been present at the Dublin meeting. Finally, Hay asserted, quite correctly, that the resolutions did the Catholic cause a great disservice.[451]

Hay's trip to London with the petition was also disrupted by financial problems. Differences between Hay and Dromgoole exacerbated an already tense environment. Hay complained to O'Connell that Dromgoole had 'not condescended even to acknowledge' the receipt of several letters Hay had written. Later he assured O'Connell 'that there were as many parties [and] petty jealousies among parliamentary folks as in our Committee, as much reviling, whispering and underhand writing as there is to be seen in minor circles'. He sought O'Connell's opinion as he valued it very much.[452] On several occasions he wrote to O'Connell, though this was to no avail. Hay complained that he received information in a 'roundabout way' and 'that was no treatment for a secretary or the deputation that possessed the confidence of the Catholic body'. Hay declared that he had been 'very badly treated'[453] according to a report by the Catholic Board. Dromgoole was requested to write to Hay in order to provide him with information. Just a month later Dromgoole resigned as acting secretary. Prophetically, he became secretary to the Finance Committee.[454] Clearly Hay was being side-lined by his former friends.

Revealingly, Hay wrote to O'Connell about the Board's finances when he returned to Dublin. He complained:

Though you did me justice in saying that my life and utmost exertions are devoted to the service of the Catholics of Ireland yet the private state of my finances would be desperate indeed if I shall be obliged to pay this demand which I had not the most distant idea of from what you stated to me. Nay, what I have already paid is already an object to me notwithstanding that Mr O'Connell has a fair demand for other charges.[455]

Hay had had been left to pay the Catholic Board's debts. Although he tried on several occasions to organise a meeting of the Committee of Accounts (of which O'Connell and Dromgoole were members), he was unsuccessful. Hay complained about the 'hardship of … being obliged to accept bills due to the newspapers'.[456] This decision is remarkable when one considers that it had been decided, in March, that the expenses of the delegates were to be paid by the Board and a financial subcommittee was appointed to organise these payments.[457] Additionally, Hay produced a list of expenses incurred by the delegation.[458] Why were the Board and Hay in financial difficulty? The Catholics incurred heavy legal expenses because of government interference in their activities. Furthermore, with the gradual desertion of the aristocrats from the Board, subscriptions dried up. Hay's financial instability was exacerbated by the demands of the Catholic Board and his family. Although no private papers appear to have survived, Edward Hay was married and had several children, according to the 1826 report in the New Catholic Association papers.[459]

While Hay was in London, Dromgoole complained that some necessary papers for the Accounts Committee were locked up. Hay was obviously insulted by this accusation and Richard O'Brien of the Accounts Committee consoled Hay by assuring him that his zeal and integrity were not in question.[460] Hay responded by emphasising that he had fulfilled his duties and left nothing undone. 'I left you the whole of the proceedings … [and] as to the accounts they speak for themselves', he asserted in a letter to Dromgoole.[461] Intriguingly, O'Connell proclaimed in a speech that Hay 'devoted his life to the service of the Irish people, and refused to receive any other recompense than what was to be found in the barren praises of his countrymen'.[462] O'Connell, who was notorious with money, presumed that Hay would willingly pay the expenses. Hay's refusal to pay the bills created grave problems for the Board. Plus the fact that he did not have a regular income placed him in a vulnerable position.

As secretary, Hay received the bills for the Board and this placed him in a very embarrassing position. Tim D'Arcy of D'Arcy's tavern, where some of the Catholic meetings were held, wrote to Hay demanding money that was owed to him for a Catholic dinner held a year earlier. D'Arcy threatened to ask Fingall for the money if the Board refused to pay.[463] Hay's only resort was to send circulars seeking funds, as he wished to be 'relieved' of the 'many demands' which were made for payment of several bills.[464] He also mentioned that the subscriptions to the Board were exhausted. Hay sarcastically admitted that he enjoyed 'the exclusive honour of being held responsible for a great part of the expenses attendant on the petitions'.[465]

Hay was not the only person put under pressure by O'Connell. Mr James Bagot of Belchamp, Coolock in north Dublin, received a letter from the subcommittee of accounts signed by O'Connell, which warned him to pay his five guineas. If he did not pay, Bagot would be prevented from managing petitions.[466] It is not known whether individual subscriptions (such as the donation of three guineas from Fr David Burke, parish priest of Rosscarbery, County Cork) given to Hay were handed over to the general account or kept by Hay.[467] His position as a treasurer made him vulnerable when there were financial difficulties. There is no doubt that the peers made a substantial contribution to the Board's finances while they were involved in the Catholic affairs. Viscount Netterville, for example, sent Hay £5 and Fingall sent £25 during 1812, but these individuals were no longer prominent on the Catholic Board.[468] To make matters worse, Dromgoole made a particularly prejudiced speech and then promptly disappeared from the scene until he resurfaced in Rome during the Rescript crisis of 1814, which will be discussed shortly. Dromgoole was replaced by O'Connell on the accounts committee.[469]

During all this adversity, Hay continued to keep the public informed about Catholic activities. A sample of his correspondence in 1812 is indicative of the perception of Hay among outsiders. William Tighe, writing from London, asked Hay to provide him with information about the conduct of Orange juries in Wexford and elsewhere. Jane McAwly from Temora was a 'regular scribbler' and often wrote to Hay for Catholic news or advice about what to do with her sons. In her customary timid style, she asked Hay to excuse her 'little scribbling' and, in a phrase revealing the era's social mores, she declared that it did not suit her sex 'to make themselves ostensible'. Nonetheless, through her regular letters to Hay she was kept informed about national news. She begged Hay to burn her correspondence, as she was fearful of being exposed. Fortunately (for history) Hay ignored her plea.

Hay was an accessible individual, as well as a source of information. Bishop Dominic Bellew of Killala sought Hay's advice when a group of Methodists were 'let loose' in his diocese, since Hay had 'exerted' himself on behalf of the Catholics.[470] Through his contacts, Hay was alerted to developments on a local and national level.

Nationally, the appointment of Robert Peel, a young, very able and determined politician, as Chief Secretary on 4 August 1812, adversely affected the Catholics. Peel was determined to impede the activities of the Catholic Board whenever possible. He was worried that conciliatory aristocrats on the Board were being replaced by aggressive O'Connellites. The mutual antagonism between Peel and O'Connell did not help Hay in his work as secretary.[471] The Committee declared at an aggregate meeting that the 'voice of [the] Assembly has reached the limits of our Island'. The fact that the voice of the Catholic body was heard was due in no small part to the energy of its secretary, Edward Hay.[472] However, internal dissension and external pressures over the next few years would lessen the impact of the Catholic Board.

HAY AND CATHOLICS IN DISARRAY

In 1813, the Catholic Board decided, yet again, to petition parliament for relief. Revealingly, the petition introduced by Grattan was only narrowly defeated in the House of Commons by 251 votes to 247. This result suggested that the various Catholic pressure groups had managed to convince many members of parliament that emancipation was worthy of support. However, the relative success of the petition hid many of the problems facing the Catholics in general, and Hay in particular. Hay had travelled to London as secretary to the delegation, but his activities in London did not endear him to some of the delegates. Peter Bodkin-Hussey, a barrister and a member of the Catholic Board, complained that Hay was acting 'as predicted'.

Self-important and belligerent, Hay insisted he was one of the delegates and was 'inclined to quarrel'. Hay subjected the delegates to 'ridicule' because of his behaviour.[473] Furthermore, Hay was not content with taking instructions from the delegates in London. He had been active in Catholic politics since the early 1790s and he valued his autonomy and position. However, the Board sought to curtail the independence of its members. Bodkin-Hussey, again writing from London, criticised Hay, who was tiring all the Board's friends 'with his tedious and tiresome visits'.[474]

Hay had always enjoyed the opportunity to converse on Catholic issues with prominent British politicians and he did not appreciate the domineering attitude of the Board. No doubt, his loquacity and indiscretion were proving to be liabilities for the Board. O'Connell proposed at a Catholic meeting that nobody be permitted to communicate with the government without the Board's authority. A week later, O'Connell repeated this resolution with the addition that, unless one was delegated to speak for the Board, no correspondence should pass between the Catholic body and the authorities.[475] O'Connell's bullying attitude and Hay's lack of discretion played their part in precipitating Hay's departure from Catholic politics.

However, criticism of Hay stemmed primarily from the financial problems of the Board. These financial problems partly derived from prosecutions against Catholic publishers, such as Hugh Fitzpatrick and John Magee of the *Dublin Evening Post*. Hugh Fitzpatrick was fined and imprisoned because he published Scully's pamphlet on the Penal Laws and John Magee was prosecuted for publishing an anti-government speech of O'Connell's. Historian Brian Inglis has suggested that O'Connell regarded the press 'as no more than ammunition in his campaign.' Catholic publishers were sacrificed for O'Connell's 'own protection'.[476] As Sean Connolly has noted, 'those whose resolutions and speeches the *Dublin Evening Post* had reported had refused to accept their share of the legal responsibility for the contents'.[477] Later events were to indicate that Hay was also a victim of O'Connell's self-preservation.

Up to mid-1813, the *Dublin Evening Post* was the Catholics' most vocal supporter, but the newspaper now became very critical of the Catholics in general. Hay was also targeted. In mid-May, there was a long editorial comment on Hay. They described him as the 'depository of Catholic Secrets and organ … of the Catholic Board in England'. The newspaper also suggested that although Hay 'was employed by the Catholic Board' he wrote as if 'he was employed by their enemies'. The *Dublin Evening Post* referred to his 'ignorance' on the question of Domestic Nomination and, more personally, his 'nondescript' appearance. The piece continued, 'Mr Hay is an excellent letter-carrier, and an indefatigable letter-reader – but let us keep him at home – he does very well to copy resolutions, though he is not equally clever at accounts.' Hay was 'utterly incompetent' and unsuited 'by nature and by education' to the post of secretary, they asserted. The *Dublin Evening Post* was annoyed that Hay disagreed with their discussion of the Catholic Bill.[478]

However, the differences between Hay and the newspaper do not fully explain the personal nature of the attack. Hay was under pressure on the Board because of its financial difficulties. Hence, he was an easy target for the newspaper's writers who wanted to criticise the Catholic Board. As the person who paid the bills, Hay was perceived to be culpable for the Catholic debts. The Catholic Board already owed money to the *Dublin Evening Post*. Its editor, Magee, languished in Newgate Gaol, yet no help was forthcoming from the Catholic Board. It could also be argued that O'Connell's dramatic 'defence' at Magee's trial, where he vilified the government, did nothing to shorten Magee's term.

In response to the attack on Hay, the Catholic Board defended his activities. The aristocrat Edward Bellew praised Hay's 'unabated assiduity, unremitted exertion, [and his] uncontaminated purity'. O'Connell repeated his earlier claim that Hay refused money for his exertions while Lord Ffrench declared that his 'friend [Hay had] … lost his family in support of Ireland'.[479] There followed numerous panegyrics on behalf of 'HONEST NED HAY' in the *Dublin Evening Post*. Yet the newspaper was not finished with its criticism of Hay and his activities in London. This ironic poem was published in the newspaper early in June:

Come home, Neddy Hay! Come home, Neddy Hay
and tell us what you did
All the time you were away!
Come home, Neddy Hay! Come home, Neddy Hay
We'll thank you if you come
and we'll thank you not to stay.
Did you see ABY BABY! Neddy Hay! Neddy Hay!
And how did he look
Upon the Levee day?
Did you see the COSSACK! Neddy Hay! Neddy Hay!
Was his Pike very long,
And his whiskers very grey?
Did you see Paddy Duggan! Neddy Hay! Neddy Hay!
Arrah does he keep a Jingle,
Or a one horse Chay?
Did you go to the Park! Did you go to the Park!

I hope you bought new Breeches,
Honest Neddy Hay?
Come home, Neddy Hay! Come home, Neddy Hay!
Between THE POST and the BISHOPS,
There's the Devil to pay!
Sure HUGHYS in Quad! Neddy Hay, Neddy Hay!
'Pon my soul, he was put in,
By the Duke of ROSCREA!!!
Before you set off Neddy Hay, Neddy Hay!
Give 'y Love to the Duke!
And to Viscount CASTLEREAGH!![480]

The *Dublin Evening Post* was clearly annoyed at the way publishers suffered on behalf of the Catholic cause, and the blame was firmly and unfairly placed on Hay's shoulders. Ironically, when Hay eventually split from O'Connell in 1818, the newspaper was very sympathetic to his fate. They were all too familiar with financial woes due, in part, to the political ambitions of others. But in 1813, in the newspaper's eyes, Hay was accountable for the Catholic debts.

An analysis of the Catholic Board's accounts sheds some interesting light on their financial arrangements. At a meeting of the Committee of Accounts in mid-June, it was noted that there was £2,144 8*s* 4*d* in the account. This was a very substantial sum of money in early nine-teenth-century Ireland. In later years Hay maintained that O'Connell kept the accounts 'under lock and key'.[481] Between 1809 and 1813 the Catholic body was in the black, financially speaking, despite spending considerable sums of money on newspaper advertisements.[482] This concurs with the view of a Catholic barrister, Randall Kiernan, who 'said in 1835 that he had been handsomely paid by the Catholic Board' to publish information. 'They had large funds for that special purpose, and he admitted that he had a very good share of them.'[483] The financial returns of the Catholics indicate that Hay usually paid the bills as 'disbursements [were] made by E. Hay' or 'per Hay'.[484] Therefore, as secretary, Hay was liable, even if he was not responsible, for the debts of the Catholic Board. The *Dublin Evening Post* believed that O'Connell's friendship with Hay 'cooled' when O'Connell became 'an active member of the Committee of Accounts'.

The newspaper suggested that Hay be 'brought over the coals' because of the accounts. The *Dublin Evening Post* also enquired if Hay really 'possessed [the] … unbounded confidence' of the Board since he was removed 'from the management of their MONEY affairs'.[485] Hay, in his defence, explained that his accounts were 'inspected'.[486] Early the following year, it was again decided to reimburse Hay for his expenses on behalf of the Catholics but this 'decision was never implemented'.[487] Given that Hay did not have a private income, his position as a treasurer made him very vulnerable.

Differences between Hay and Troy also created problems. A letter from Donoughmore to Troy convinced Hay that the Archbishop was willing to accept some clauses in the Catholic Bill. Troy denied this and accused Hay of misconceiving what he had written.[488] Furthermore, the publication of Monsignor Quarantotti's Rescript,[489] which stated that it was 'highly proper that our prelates should be agreeable and acceptable to the King' thereby giving the King a negative veto over episcopal appointments, also upset the Catholic Board.[490] At a Catholic meeting, a 'private' letter between Hay and Donoughmore was read. Hay was annoyed that his private views were made known to the meeting. A week later it was decided that the correspondence of the Board would be referred to the Committee of Accounts.[491]

Hay's friendship with Donoughmore caused problems, as he became further distanced from the 'power brokers' on the Board. Both of them disliked the domineering attitude of the barristers, such as Scully and O'Connell, and they both favoured domestic nomination of bishops. Furthermore, by 1813 the hierarchy was depleted; the dioceses of Tuam, Elphin, Cashel, Cork, Killala, Limerick, Kildare and Leighlin, Ardagh and Ossory were without bishops.[492]

The clandestine correspondence between Hay and Donoughmore during 1815-1816 makes clear Hay's split with O'Connell and his frustration with the lack of progress of the Catholics.[493] Donoughmore described the Board as a 'debating society'. However, as he explained to his brother Francis Hely-Hutchinson:

> … [in the] midst of all this insanity, one man always appears to have never lost his head – I mean Edward Hay, in whom there is a great deal of directness of conduct, a great deal of real firmness, and a great deal of friendly feeling towards all of us. I should be glad he was apprised that such are truly and sincerely, my sentiments upon his subject …[494]

A month later, in January of 1814, Donoughmore informed Hay that their ideas 'both of person and of things chime'.[495] Despite this vote of confidence, Hay was to face further difficulties.

HAY'S TRIBULATIONS WORSEN

The year 1814 brought no joy for Hay. Despite a motion to consider Hay's long services as secretary (which carries with it the implication that Hay's work was not awarded already) nothing was done to compensate Hay for his efforts.[496] A couple of months later, O'Connell praised Hay's work on behalf of the Catholics and his 'devotion to the interests of his Countrymen'. O'Connell believed that the 'Board had enjoyed [Hay's] … services long enough without remuneration'.[497] But Hay's minutes of the meetings tell their own story. On 5 March, Hay arrived and there was no meeting, and on 12 and 19 March there were not enough members to constitute a quorum. On 12 April there were still insufficient numbers for a quorum.[498]

What had happened to the Catholic cause? The gradual departure of the peers, the continuing saga of the Veto and the ever-present financial problems all militated against any progress being made by the Catholics. Lord Ffrench's bank, where the Catholic accounts were lodged, collapsed in 1814. Hay's correspondence with Ffrench seven years previously suggests that he had a personal account in the bank. Hay asked Ffrench to 'discount my Bill for that sum and as a security I leave you the Bond I lodged for £2,000'.[499] If Hay's account was at Ffrench's bank then his personal finances must have been in a very poor state following the bank's collapse.

Despite all these disruptions, Hay continued to correspond with individuals interested in the Catholic question. He was asked to dispel rumours about the English Catholics who received a bad press in Ireland thanks to Bishop Milner. Will you 'do all in your power to undeceive the public in Ireland, as to the pretended Catholic meeting in England', Jerningham pleaded.[500] Donoughmore asked Hay 'what the general sentiment was on the idea … of not agitating'.[501] The ever-supportive Fingall promised to help Hay with the accounts and he felt sure that the general body appreciated the secretary's 'merits'.[502] Fingall's home was used for a Catholic meeting late in 1814. The volume of Hay's correspondence declined as the Catholic body became less active. The inertia was precipitated by the suppression of the Catholic Board by vice-regal proclamation in June 1814.

By that time, there was 'not a shilling' in the Board's treasury, according to Hay.[503] The Board had become a 'noisy and disreputable debating club'.[504] *The Cork Mercantile Chronicle*, in a reference to the financial problems of the Catholic body, claimed that the Board was 'a Drama, of which, Physicians without Fees, Lawyers without Briefs, Shopkeepers without Business, Captains without Commissions, and Bankrupts without Certificates, were the component characters'.[505] Despite these difficulties, the Catholic Association was formed in 1815.

HAY AND THE CATHOLIC ASSOCIATION

An aggregate meeting on 24 January 1815 decided to form a Catholic Association.[506] This did not mean that there was a complete change in the activities or members of the previous Catholic body. The name was changed so that the Catholics could still operate without violating the 1793 Convention Act. The problems facing the Association were exactly the same as those the Board tried to grapple with. In March, Hay was appointed secretary. Interestingly, O'Connell proposed that the secretary should not correspond with anyone on Catholic affairs 'without the sanction of the Committee' or the Association.[507] This deprived Hay of the freedom to seek out information on issues that pertained to the Catholics. It also reflects O'Connell's desire to control the Association. Clearly he did not trust Hay.

Hay's pestering of individuals and his tendency to consort with prominent politicians worried O'Connell, as the former was inclined to be indiscreet. For example, Hay's strong views on episcopal organisation did not endear him to the hierarchy. This was impolitic, as bishops needed to be courted by the Association. Secular leaders who sought to influence ecclesiastical affairs were ridiculed by members of the hierarchy. Bishop Power wondered what influence the Catholic leaders had on the people and he wrote that the government laughed at their '*soi-disant* importance'.[508] In contrast, the *Dublin Evening Post* declared that the Catholics met once a week, their meetings consisted of 500 individuals and the organisation 'virtually represented the sentiments of the Catholics'.[509] Archbishop Troy, despite differences with the Association over episcopal nominations, gave the Catholics the use of any chapel in Dublin for their meetings.[510] Hence, members of the hierarchy were willing to facilitate the Catholic Association, though they were unwilling to let them influence ecclesiastical politics.

In later years, Hay wrote that his main duty as secretary was the arrangement of the petition to parliament.[511] Once this task had been dealt with, Hay was an independent operator. Clearly he did not like being impeded by O'Connell. In this way, his views chimed with Donoughmore, who did not appreciate being 'dictated to' by prominent Catholics. In 1815, Donoughmore refused 'to submit to the degradation of becoming the Parliamentary Automation of any man'.[512] Despite differences with O'Connell, Hay was still committed to the Catholic cause. At a Catholic Association meeting in February it was decided that, in order to encourage membership, gentlemen could enter their names in a book at 4 Capel Street. Hay ensured that the book was available 'from 11 to 3 each day' so that as many individuals as possible could sign their names.[513]

It is clear then that Hay was proceeding with his work. In a circular, he made clear his commitment to the Catholic cause. He supported domestic nomination of bishops and his desire to communicate the proceedings of the Catholic body to the country at large ensured that he memorised the names of people who were interested in the Catholic cause. Furthermore, he availed of businessmen in Dublin who were a 'source of invaluable information'.[514] Clearly Hay saw himself as the supreme networker on behalf of the Catholics of Ireland.

The letters received by Hay during 1815 indicate that, despite apparent lack of political progress, the Association was as busy as ever. Favours were still sought from Hay from those who perceived him as influential. David O'Callaghan, from Carlow College, the Catholic seminary, asked Hay to use his 'influence' to obtain letters of recommendation for Theodore O'Callaghan, who was in the army. In return, O'Callaghan promised to obtain the 'names of the priests of the diocese of Kildare and Leighlin'.[515] Lots of individuals asked Hay for financial loans which is remarkable considering his financial position. Hay was also asked to publicise local events in the national newspapers. Donoughmore praised Hay's position as the 'only permanent officer' of the Catholic body. Impatient, Donoughmore was resentful of the 'dictators' who were 'mere talkers' and he described them as 'shabby agitators'.[516] Hay may have thought that he was left with all the work, while the prominent members of the Association sprouted rhetoric.

The responses to Hay's communications also shed some light on the financial situation of the Association. Bishop James

O'Shaughnessy of Killaloe, in a reply to Hay's circular, sent five guineas towards the debts of the Association.[517] Fingall sent £50 and a couple of months later he wrote that he would send Hay the money he needed. Fingall also wished that Catholic gratitude to Hay would be made tangible.[518] It is clear that Hay was left with the responsibility of paying the ever-increasing Catholic debts.

Hay's personal finances were exacerbated by the lawsuit against his brother Philip. The secretary wrote to his cousin in Ross with the following information, 'I have renewed my suit against my brother and I must obtain a final decree next time so that I shall then be enabled to be more comfortable than I have been for some time past.' Later he asked his cousin to collect funds for the testimonial organised to honour him. This, Hay felt, would 'honour the Hay name'. Hay complained that O'Connell was a 'dictator'. Several months later Hay maintained that he had received the 'benefit of the decree' against his brother but he could not command his brother's payment.[519] Hence, Hay's financial vulnerability was all the more frustrating.

To make matters even worse, in 1815, the Association decided to send a deputation to Rome to present the Irish laity's views against the Veto. Richard Hayes, a Franciscan monk from Wexford, was the deputation's secretary. Over the next two years Hayes managed to alienate influential individuals in Rome. Finally, he demanded expenses from the Catholic Association for his stay in Italy.[520] Not surprisingly, this money was not forthcoming and Hay felt the full impact of Hayes's frustrations.

LAST YEARS AS SECRETARY

The last three years of Hay's active involvement in the Catholic Association (1816-18) were dominated by economic and ecclesiastical difficulties. The Catholics reached their lowest ebb and Peel triumphantly declared in 1816, 'we have no Catholic Board – nor any factious association under any denomination – no aggregate meetings – no itinerant orators – and what is much better – there is no apparent disposition to receive them with any sort of applause or encouragement.'[521] Hay was affected by these setbacks.

Richard Hayes was expelled from Rome in 1817 but not before Patrick Hayes (Richard's brother) had accused Hay of being a 'time-serving fellow'. The disagreements between Richard Hayes and Hay related to the fact that Hay refused to accept a letter from Hayes because it was not officially addressed to the secretary.[522] The antagonism between the two stemmed in part from Hay's belief that the money Hayes sought should have been used to pay the outstanding debts of the Catholic body. When Hayes returned to Ireland he demanded £840 from the Catholics for expenses. Inevitably, he never received any money. The unseemly row between Hay and Hayes, as well as the latter's behaviour in Rome, did nothing for the Irish Catholic's cause on the international stage.

The divisions caused by the whole Veto controversy were clearly evident from the fact that there were two Catholic petitions in 1817: one supporting the Veto from Lord Trimbleston and his supporters, and the other from the Catholic Association. Hay and the Catholic Association still sought some form of domestic nomination. Hay even wrote to Pope Pius VII and asked him to 'protect Catholic interests in Ireland by allowing episcopal appointments to become "perfectly domestic" … thus insuring [*sic*] Roman confirmation to the person elected'.[523] Hay emphasised this viewpoint to Donoughmore:

> No greater misfortune to the Catholic cause than that the bishops should become electors of their own body. The establishment of deans and chapters, properly acted upon, would justly circumscribe the rights of the bishops, as well as those of the second order of the clergy.[524]

However, no matter how much correspondence was generated, the bishops were not willing to allow any form of ecclesiastical home rule.

The correspondence between Hay and Donoughmore also contained many critical references to the 'would-be dictators' Scully and O'Connell.[525] Hay was under attack from O'Connell because of the Association's financial problems. Moreover, O'Connell criticised Hay for not publishing the bishops' anti-Veto letters.[526] In 1824, Hay wrote that years earlier O'Connell delivered to him 'a schedule of the Debts on account of the Catholics of Ireland' which amounted to £1,482.[527] The Association had frittered away money on their new newspaper the *Chronicle*, which was edited by Eneas O'Donnell. The editor, like Hay, eventually split from O'Connell. Even Scully was at odds with O'Connell, because the Tipperary barrister was owed £2,274 in 1817.

Scully was still seeking his money in 1822.[528] Nonetheless, despite O'Connell's willingness to use friends as temporary bankers, Hay received all the blame for the Catholic debts.

In November 1818, Hay wrote to the *Dublin Evening Post*. He explained that he was liable to arrest for debts incurred as secretary to the Catholics of Ireland. 'Law proceedings have been instituted against me, for a Public Debt', Hay complained.[529] His predicament brought a sympathetic response from some quarters. Troy sent money because of his 'personal regard and feeling' for Hay.[530] A small committee (most of whose members were part of the Catholic Association) was established to help Hay, as he was 'personally liable' for the debts.[531] Meanwhile, O'Connell declared, 'The [Catholic] Board is defunct. Honest Ned has outlawed us all. He makes no distinctions. There are many debts due – there is a great indisposition to organise.'[532] O'Connell did not take any responsibility for any of the difficulties faced by the Catholic Association.

Hay was a high-profile and respected figure at the beginning of the 1810s. However, by the end of the decade he was deposed from his position as secretary to the Catholic Association. His extensive journeys in Ireland and abroad, as well as his attempts to keep in contact with the mood of the Catholic nation, culminated in bankruptcy and despair. Hay's dream of 'a permanent Committee holding Communication with the different parts of Ireland in order to obtain satisfactory and constant intelligence … [on] the merits of the case of the Catholics of Ireland' was shattered by factors over which he had little control.[533]

However, Hay's efforts were not entirely in vain. Embryonic representation manifested itself on the Catholic Committee. In time, this Catholic Committee grew into the Catholic Association. Hay played an important part in the creation of an audience receptive to political ideas. Ironically, it was O'Connell who was to benefit most from the hidden work of Hay and others in the early stages of overt Catholic agitation. When Hay proved to be a useful scapegoat for the financial problems of the Catholics, O'Connell renounced one of the more energetic Catholic activists. Many years later, O'Connell admitted that Hay was 'doing the business of the nation'.[534]

VI

A SERVANT OF EIGHT
MILLION PEOPLE, 1820-1826

The last eight years of Hay's life were characterised by bitter disillusionment. Disagreements with 'old friends' ensured that Hay was
at the centre of various public controversies. Hay's eventual exile
in Kilmainham Gaol and his death in total penury provide a most
inappropriate conclusion to the career of one of the most industrious and long-standing Catholic activists.

SECRET COMMUNICATIONS

A Catholic meeting in March 1819 requested that Hay act as
secretary. Fingall praised Hay and the secretary was elected
unanimously.[535] However, by July a row had broken out between
O'Connell and Hay over a secret communication between Hay and
a member of the British cabinet. The secret communication related
to the involvement of the opposition in the 'Witchery Resolutions'
of 1812. Hay had communicated with a 'parliamentary friend upon
the subject' and his letter suggested that the Witchery Resolutions
were 'prepared by the Opposition'.[536]

At the Catholic meeting, Hay refused to produce the letter he
had written. It is clear that he had communicated with Canning
(a member of the opposition as well as a supporter of Catholic
emancipation) and offered some 'explanations' about the input
of the Catholic body or their innocence during the 1812 resolutions.[537] O'Connell argued that Hay's information was a 'gross
falsehood' but Hay insisted that the Catholics had nothing to do
with the resolutions in 1812 and the original resolutions of the
Catholics had been changed.[538] O'Connell naturally wanted to
protect the Whigs and Ponsonby from any possible allegations

about the resolutions. Hence, he was very embarrassed when Hay leaked this information.

Why did Hay release this information seven years after the event? There are two possible reasons. First, he wished to clear the names of the Catholics. Secondly, it was an attempt to disconcert Scully and O'Connell, who had most to lose from Hay's revelations.

In a letter to the *Dublin Evening Post*, Hay made it clear that he had stayed in London after the 1812 petition in order to supervise the publication of the parliamentary debates on Catholic petitions. 'I had interviews [he wrote] at that time with almost every one of our Irish Parliamentary Supporters', and Hay wanted the Catholic body to be exonerated 'from the charge of any intentional offence against their Sovereign'. He also admitted to 'conversations with members of the Legislature' which were 'purely confidential'.[539] A month later, both O'Connell and Scully denied that they had communicated with the opposition about the 'Witchery Resolutions'.[540] O'Connell declared that Hay had 'acted on idle report, or vague and visionary conjecture … it was very drivelling and dotage of composition, and required no reply'.[541] The *Dublin Evening Post* had questioned the truth of O'Connell's statements and O'Connell, in turn, accused the paper of calumny. By this stage, Hay's estrangement from O'Connell and the Catholic Association was virtually complete.

Hay's old friend and mutual antagonist of O'Connell, Lord Donoughmore, also rejected him. Donoughmore naturally, like O'Connell, did not want to upset the Whigs who were the allies of the Catholics. Donoughmore and his brother Francis Hely-Hutchinson parted with Hay as a result of his revelations about the actual origin the resolutions.[542] As old friends parted, so old enemies became new friends. O'Connell informed his wife that he had:

> … a very flattering communication from Lord Donoughmore on the subject of the resolutions of 1812. He seems actually delighted with my conduct and is certainly inflamed with a great rage against "honest Ned Hay". That scoundrel can never show his ugly nose and dirty person in Catholic affairs…[543]

It is understandable that Donoughmore and O'Connell were on good terms. Neither of them wanted to antagonise an important Whig like Ponsonby, and Hay was no longer considered a worthwhile ally. Hay, in his defence, declared that O'Connell's logic deserted him when he left the Four Courts. He also believed that it was the 'right of [a] private person to expose the errors of men in public situations'. Hay argued that his job was 'confined to conveying communication from Catholic meetings to individuals and the public and conveying communication from individuals and the public to Catholic meetings.'[544] This, Hay concluded, entitled him to converse as a private person with individuals on Catholic issues without jeopardising his position as secretary.

A Committee of Investigation on Hay's conduct was established to ascertain the veracity of the allegations against Hay. Impatiently, O'Connell wanted a declaration of the charges 'on the spot'. The two charges against Hay were: first, that he had written to Canning about the Witchery Resolutions, and second, that he had communicated with the *Dublin Evening Post*. O'Connell again emphasised that the resolutions had not emanated from British Whig politician Ponsonby.[545] Hay argued at length about his right as a private citizen to write to a Cabinet Minister.[546] O'Connell, on the other hand, maintained that the inquiry related 'to a public man upon public business'.[547]

In yet another letter to the *Dublin Evening Post*, Hay insisted that he had never mentioned Ponsonby to Canning and he did not appreciate O'Connell's 'dictatorial' approach to the Committee of Investigation. Hay felt it should not be turned into a 'Public Inquisitorial Tribunal'.[548] In late February 1820, Hay was vindicated by the testimonial of the Court of Honour. Unfortunately, this did not signal his return to the Catholic Association.

The Committee of Investigation affair illustrates two factors which affected Hay in his later years as secretary. First, he always felt that he was free to communicate with whomever he wanted in order to further the cause of Catholic emancipation. His letter to Canning was undoubtedly motivated by a desire to undermine the influences of O'Connell and Scully. More importantly, Hay wanted to clear the name of the Catholic body in relation to the Witchery Resolutions. Secondly, throughout the 1810s, O'Connell's domineering personality refused to 'tolerate any diversity of opinion'. 'The Liberator' was also willing to use the press when it suited him. Hay suffered because he was not prepared to change the habits of three decades in Catholic politics. Hay, at nearly sixty years of age, was not enthusiastic about taking orders from younger men like O'Connell.

While languishing in Kilmainham, Hay was prevented by O'Connell from publishing his version of the affair. The *Dublin Morning Post* proclaimed:

> …we are compelled to withdraw the promised letter of Mr Hay, unless we have the leave of Mr O'Connell to publish it, as we apprehend it contains matter which that Gentleman, in his zeal for free discussion, may deem sufficient to enable him to commence a second prosecution against the Proprietor of the *Dublin Morning Post* …[549]

O'Connell was not going to let his reputation be tarnished – even if that meant prosecuting newspapers. Hay, writing from Kilmainham, explained that 'to hector and to bully, to threaten and to indict, would sound well in the area of the Four Courts, but will avail little to conceal from an impanelled Jury, or the free sentiments of an impartial public' the truth of the case. He felt he had 'suffered from the professed friendship and interposition of Mr O'Connell'.[550] Hay was confined to Kilmainham Debtors' Gaol between 19 January and 11 March 1822.[551] Even after his release it was very difficult for him to clear his own name unless he had access to the newspapers. In a letter (written on the back of an 1814 circular) to the editor of *Saunder's Newsletter*, Hay protested that he was under obligation to O'Connell and he had 'no means of displaying the truth'.[552]

CATHOLIC DEBTS AND DOMESTIC NOMINATION

The communication between Hay and Canning was not the only contentious issue between O'Connell and Hay. The fundamental question of accountability and the debts of the Catholics was aired in public. The *Dublin Morning Post* assured its readers that when Hay 'transferred the accounts of the Catholic Board into the hands of Mr O'Connell, there was a cash balance of £695-15-7 then standing to the credit of the Catholics of Ireland, certified by the Committee of Accounts'.[553] The *Dublin Morning Post* asserted that Hay never meddled with the accounts, as they were kept by O'Connell:

> No man [the newspaper wrote] ever Laboured more sedulously and more honestly in the cause of the Catholics than Mr Hay; he spent

his life in their service; and ruined his fortune; perhaps, by relying on the hollow professions of some false friend.[554]

Hay even maintained that O'Connell kept £40 belonging to the Catholics. He wrote that he had never received remuneration for his 'long and faithful services' and that Orangemen were more honourable than O'Connell, a very damning denunciation considering Hay's experiences with Orangemen in Wexford.[555]

O'Connell naturally denied Hay's 'allegations'. He dismissed Hay as being 'unintelligible' and he declared that 'every sixpence [belonging to the Catholic body] was disposed of'. Revealingly, when O'Connell was appointed secretary of the Accounts Committee he ceased to be friends with Hay.[556] Interestingly, when several newspapers approached the 'New' Catholic Association (which had been established in 1824) for reimbursements due to them, O'Connell declared that the debts were due from a different Catholic body.[557] Technically, this was correct, but many prominent individuals of the Catholic Association were members of the New Catholic Association. The money was still owed to the newspapers. As Brian Inglis has pointed out, the charges 'that the Association owed upwards of £1,000 to certain newspapers were explained away by O'Connell as debts contracted by the Catholic Board'. O'Connell avowed that the Association, therefore, had 'nothing to do with the debts of the Catholic Board'.[558] This is all the more remarkable when one considers that in the 1820s, O'Connell and the Catholic Association spent £15,000 annually influencing the press.[559] If the powerful press were unsuccessful in gaining a redress of their grievances, then there was little hope for Hay.

However, Hay still had his friends from his long involvement in Catholic politics. Charles Finn of Carlow (a member of the Catholic Association, and son of Thomas Finn, who had been acting secretary of the Catholic Committee) wrote to Hay regarding the financial transactions of the Catholic body. Considerable sums of money had been received by the Catholics, and Finn, intriguingly, wanted to know how much money was paid to the lawyers during the various trials and prosecutions against Catholic publishers. Unfortunately we do not have the answer to this question. Nevertheless, the fact that the inquiry was made suggests that certain lawyers benefited from the cases taken by various newspapers.

Apart from Hay's letters from Kilmainham, very little is known about Hay's sojourn in gaol. An antagonistic observer of Hay revealed that Hay indulged in oratory early in the morning and his appearance was 'that of an exasperated ruffian'. The writer did admit that Hay advanced his money towards the support of the Catholics and he 'got himself into Prison for debt incurred by his action' on behalf of the Catholics.[560]

Despite all his difficulties, Hay was involved in two of his hobbies: ecclesiastical controversy (particularly his preference for the domestic nomination of bishops) and writing history. Early in 1822, a series of letters appeared in the *Dublin Evening Post* by Hay and JKL (James Warren Doyle, Bishop of Kildare and Leighlin). As usual, Hay was setting forth the advantages of domestic nomination of the bishops through enabling the Dean and Chapter of the diocese. His letter from Camden Street in Dublin suggested that if the bishops agreed to the 'confirmation of the Rights of the second Order of the Clergy, the Dean and Chapter', they would thereby remove 'a bar to the emancipation of the Catholics of Ireland'.[561] This form of nomination would also 'prevent the bishops from meddling in politics'. Hay blamed the bishops for the reintroduction of the Veto in 1808 as he believed they 'connived with MPs in 1808'.[562]

Hay was not alone in his criticism of the bishops. In 1817, O'Connell had criticised Troy, and, to a lesser extent, Dr Murray, his coadjutor, for their refusal to countenance domestic nomination and their acceptance of the Veto. O'Connell sneered, 'I perceive the "pliant Trojan" [Troy] has got Dr Murray's support for the Veto. Their publication of their letter to you [Hay] was intended to intimidate other bishops from that zealous opposition to the Veto which the people look for and the times require.' O'Connell was also critical of Troy's 'notorious' traffic with the Castle.[563] Subsequently, O'Connell was annoyed when Hay published the letter and thereby exposed 'The Liberator'. O'Connell maintained that the letter was written in haste and not meant for publication. The politically astute O'Connell did not want a public disagreement with the hierarchy.

Hay, however, seemed to relish his verbal and literary clashes with the hierarchy. Nevertheless, in JKL he met his match. The Bishop of Kildare and Leighlin supported a limited form of domestic nomination:

> I condole with Mr Hay, for I have known him for many years, and
> have been intimate through life with many members of his highly

respectable family, men who, if they could consider what is passing here
below, would feel sorrow and indignation (could it enter Heaven) that
their descendant could be rebuked for attacking Catholic Prelates, or
reproached with a breach of private confidence.[564]

Fitzpatrick, the bishop's biographer, was all too aware of Hay's
'self-possession and epistolary power' and his 'protest against the
continuance of any correspondence between Archbishop Troy and
the Castle'.[565] JKL eventually won the debate but the disagreement
reappeared in 1824.

Hay wrote to JKL in June 1824, and he alleged that Doyle's episcopal nomination came through British connections in Rome. In a
note at the top of the letter Doyle announced, 'I have written to Mr
Hay to deny in the most express terms every word … [as Hay's assertions were] totally untrue.' Hay concluded that there was not '*now* …
any serious difference of opinion' between himself and JKL.[566] Hay's
disagreement with JKL did not arise from any personal animosity
between the two. Rather it was Hay's determination to 'nationalise'
episcopal nominations. In this way British and Roman influence
would no longer be a factor in the selection of the hierarchy.

While this domestic nomination controversy raged, Hay
informed the *Dublin Evening Post* that he had 'long entertained the
project of publishing an historical account of Catholic Affairs of
Ireland'.[567] It would have been *The Fall and Rise of the Irish Nation*
for the early nineteenth century. Hay's historical aspirations did
not, unfortunately, move beyond the initial draft. Over 200 pages of
notes have survived, but they are in such a fragile state that they are
difficult to read.[568] Hay began with the Treaty of Limerick of 1691
and the exploits of St Ruth (the French general who fought during
the Williamite Wars in Ireland) in his proposed history. Of more
relevance to his own life, he also mentioned the United Irishmen.
He maintained that they were '25,000' strong but it was 'beneath
the dignity of Mr Hay to attend any … meeting of the society'.
Referring to his native Wexford and the build up to 1798, he refers
to the problems in the malting trade. Inevitably, Hay was critical
of Ryan (the Bishop of Ferns), O'Connell and Dromgoole. Ryan,
he believed, enjoyed government 'influence'. Hay reiterated his
conviction that the prelates should abstain from political activities.
Domestic nomination was favoured because it would 'annihilate
any idea of foreign influence'. The accounts of various Catholic

bodies were discussed. Hay declared that O'Connell audited his own accounts. The secretary 'certainly was duped'.[569]

Hay's 'history' also referred to his personal financial predicament. Hay claimed that O'Connell gave him poor legal advice about the lease of land (probably in Wexford) and the error of this advice was not discovered until 1820.[570] There appears to have been difficulties between Hay and some Wexford individuals. In the aforementioned letter of Hay to JKL there is a reference to Nicholas Sweetman of Ross. Hay claimed that the 'machinations' of Sweetman deprived him of his 'liberty for nearly five months'.[571]

Hay visited Wexford regularly, though he was based most of the time in Dublin. This prompts the question of accommodation. His brother Philip was serving in the British army on the continent during much of the Napoleonic Wars. From 1807, Philip had leased the Hay estate to the Maher family (who were originally from Tipperary and whose descendants were still living in Ballinkeele House in the 1990s). The Maher family became outright owners in 1825.[572] Hay's mother 'died at the seat of her son Philip in June 1816', according to Madden, so Edward Hay and his family may have stayed with her.[573] According to a list of the tenants on the Maher residence in 1825, Hay rented land at Ballinkeele.[574] Philip Hay was seemingly unable to sell the land until the Hay action was cleared in the courts. As late as June 1825, a deed declared that £2,106 3s 2d 'was decreed due unto Edward Hay charged and chargeable upon the lands of Ballinkeele'.[575]

Whatever about the legal intricacies of the Hay versus Hay case, the reality for Edward Hay's family, in particular his wife Winifred, was dismal. In 1826, the family was living in total penury. His first two children, a son James (who did not want to be named) and a daughter Mary-Ann were the only ones who had been educated. Louisa and Sophia, aged nineteen and seventeen, were very delicate, and William, aged fourteen, had suffered from a fever and was 'mentally impaired'. The youngest children, Caroline (aged eleven) and Edward (aged nine) were not ill, but they lived in poverty with the rest of the family.[576] Information on Hay's family only came to light when Hay died and it was decided to collect subscriptions for the family. Despite the impressive number of letters to and by Hay which have survived (over 1,000 in all), there are no letters concerning Hay's immediate family. His wife Winifred seems to have disappeared from history.

HAY'S DEATH

Hay died on Friday 13 October 1826. According to the minutes of the Catholic Association, he died from blood poisoning when a cut to his finger would not heal. The surgeon, Wright, reported to the Catholic meeting of Saturday 14 October the circumstances of Hay's death. According to Wright, Hay and his family lived 'in obscure lodgings in Dublin'. According to the *Wexford Evening Post*, Hay died in Clanbrassil Street.[577] Wright referred to the fact that Hay was entitled to a considerable property but that the disagreements between the two brothers 'threw the business into Chancery; [and] from the delays in which Court he [Hay] became considerably embarrassed for many years previous to his death. He died in absolute want, unable to procure medicines.'

The family's last blanket had been taken by the bailiff. Hay had cut himself while chopping down a tree for firewood. Wright told the meeting that Hay was, until his death, 'living upon the bounty of a few friends' who had loaned Hay money in the belief that he would receive what he was owed from his brother.[578] The *Freeman's Journal* echoed this report by stating that Hay had been supported 'by the contributions of his friends'. Furthermore, they suggested that Hay was the 'victim to the cause of his own country'. He 'had thus made personal sacrifices to his country'. They also described Hay as a faithful public servant. An 'honester hearted man never embarked on public business', they affirmed. Almost inevitably, panegyrics regarding Hay abounded once he had died.[579]

The *Dublin Evening Post* repeated the news heard at the Catholic meeting. A 'small pittance' was left to Hay but 'he was at Law with his brother for years, and never got a shilling of it. We trust it is not necessary to speak of the claims of this family upon the Catholics.'[580] The Catholic Association decided to take up a collection on behalf of the Hay family. They gave £20 towards defraying the cost of the funeral. But in an echo of earlier differences over accounts, it was decided not to use the Catholic Rent. At this stage, the rent was bringing in thousands of pounds. Instead, a committee was established to collect subscriptions on behalf of Hay's family.[581] Former Lord Lieutenants Fitzwilliam and Bedford donated £25 to the Hay family fund.[582]

The most extensive report of Hay's death appears in Madden. A hagiographical tone dominates the extract devoted to Hay:

> Edward Hay, the honest, able, indefatigable, and disinterested sup-
> porter of the Catholic cause for three-and-thirty years, the secretary
> of various associations for the emancipation of the Roman Catholics
> of Ireland for nearly twenty years, was suffered to perish in absolute
> want and misery in Dublin …

The writer then went on to describe Hay's pitiful existence before his death. Madden, who was born in 1798, had 'a very lively rec-ollection of his [Hay's] reiterated complaints, loud and bitter, of the base ingratitude with which his services to the Catholic cause had been treated', as Hay was in the 'habit of dining weekly' with Madden's father, Edward.

The last word on Hay's death is left to his old nemesis O'Connell. Hay, declared O'Connell, 'succeeded for his country, but failed for himself … He devoted the most important years of his life to their [the Catholics'] cause, years which, had he devoted to some mercan-tile pursuit, he might have rendered himself independent.' Despite Hay's desire to be reimbursed for Catholic expenses, O'Connell still persisted with the view that Hay was 'too proud to ask for relief'. A decade earlier, Hay had asked for relief but he was rebuffed. The long-serving secretary had been left responsible for the debts of the Catholics, even though he never received any compensation for expenses incurred on their behalf. O'Connell promised to obtain help for Hay's family and he revealed, 'It shall be the first symp-tom of the political regeneration of this country that the nation's gratitude is bestowed on the nation's servants.' O'Connell's offen-sive insincerity was all too evident. The *Freeman's Journal* reported the death of Winifred Hay, Hay's wife at Peter Street, Dublin, in April 1840. She was fifty-eight years old. In the 1850s, two of Hay's daughters were living in 'absolute indigence' in Dublin.[583]

VII

CONCLUSION

'I will a round unvarnished tale deliver'

> Othello in *Othello*, Act I, Scene iii,
> quoted in the introduction to Hay's *History*.

'Reputation is an idle and most false imposition, oft got without merit and lost without deserving'

> Iago in *Othello*, Act II, Scene iii.

Did Edward Hay honestly believe that his tale of 1798 was unvarnished or even accurate? It seems ironic, in retrospect, that a play that is concerned, amongst other matters, with professional jealousy between two soldiers, Othello and Iago, should form the preface to a partisan history.[584] Hay's career was both moulded and restrained by the professional aspirations of others. His work as a Catholic activist was impeded by financial and political incompetence, both his own and those of others. Furthermore, his support for the ideals of the United Irishmen set in train a long involvement in Irish public life. Undoubtedly, Hay's ill-concealed jealously towards political heavyweights such as O'Connell ensured that he joined the ever-expanding pantheon of losers in Irish history.[585] Furthermore, while O'Connell's star has not lost its lustre, Hay's reputation has dipped, or worse, he was subjected to false assumptions. Few have heard of Hay; O'Connell is one of the stars of nineteenth-century Ireland. Reputations are always fluid, however. New documentation will constantly present an individual in a different light.

Hay, who seems to have disappeared from Irish history, can be compared and contrasted with both Tone and O'Connell. Tone, like Hay, was secretary to the Catholic Committee. Like Hay, he was noted for his energetic letter writing and he realised that Catholic mobilisation could only occur if the ground was 'prepared by a writing campaign'. Both were ambassadors for Ireland and their persistent travelling on behalf of the Catholics was testament to their commitment to emancipation.[586] Elliott has described Tone as follows, 'he was no public leader, rarely initiated policy and spent much of his political career in Ireland writing service documents. Though widely recognised as the Catholics' chief publicist, his name all but disappears from government documentation for this period.' Tone was content to fold circulars and be a 'stage-hand'.[587] Hay, too, performed the crucial, if frequently unnoticed, behind-the-scenes work for the Catholics. As it transpired, both men were owed considerable sums of money for their efforts by the Catholic body.[588] However, Tone was likeable and self-deprecating whereas Hay was self-important and boastful.

Hay became a forgotten figure because of the dominance of O'Connell. The traditional history of the early years of the nineteenth century is familiar to most people. D. George Boyce has claimed that, 'Catholic needs and aspirations were given organisation and direction by Daniel O'Connell'. K.T. Hoppen has reinforced this perception by suggesting that 'by 1824 O'Connell had succeeded in transforming the small and exclusive Catholic Association, established the previous year, into something entirely novel: a broad movement with a real and effective presence throughout the whole of Catholic Ireland'.[589] The significance of Hay, or indeed anybody else who was involved in earlier Catholic bodies, has been ignored. The likes of Denys Scully, described by Thomas Wyse, the first historian of the Catholic Association, as someone who was not 'ostensibly before the Catholic public, yet no man more thoroughly governed it',[590] has, until recently, been overshadowed by O'Connell. Hay was, like Scully, a hidden power on the Catholic body. Again like Scully, he broke with O'Connell (who managed to break with everybody eventually) primarily because of money. In 1822, O'Connell owed Scully over £2,000. It could be argued that O'Connell owed much to Hay, both financially and politically.

Peter Jupp has suggested that 'O'Connell did not innovate an organisation of the Catholic vote; the ground work has been well prepared for him'.[591] It was Hay who tried to make the Catholic body as representative as possible and in this way he helped mobilise the Catholic vote. His contacts with Catholics all over the country helped broaden the base of the Catholic organisation. Hay was a sort of database for the Catholics. In 1817, he declared:

> … the source of information, that proves to me most invaluable arises from the information I receive from the traders and shop-keepers from every city and town in Ireland … they are, on many occasions, the bearers of communications of clergymen and others … thus I have been able to command a mass of intelligence hitherto uncultivated.[592]

Hay's earlier experiences, particularly as a census taker, were a great help to the Catholic body in the signing of petitions to parliament. Even Hay's involvement in the rebellion was an advantage, as this was seen as a badge of honour. Hay's *History* gave Catholics a sense of collective grievance, which only reinforced their sense of solidarity.

Hay, as noted in chapter two, was a member of his county's politicised elite. However, the 'overwhelming emphasis on the O'Connell mystique has overshadowed this bulwark – an autonomous and educated source of Catholic political activism and the cutting edge of the emancipation campaign'.[593] Hay inevitably had less of an impact on the illiterate class in Ireland but even they were affected by the emphasis on petitioning during the 1810s.

Hay's role in the politicisation and mobilisation of Irish Catholics can be measured from the changes which occurred in his lifetime. Hay was born before any of the Penal Laws had been repealed. By 1826, the Catholics were on the verge of emancipation. This transformation did not begin with the formation of the New Catholic Association in 1823.

Hay was the pulse of earlier Catholic organisations and he helped to alert the Catholics to an awareness of their disabilities. Earlier attempts at dealing with the Catholic issue had, in the words of Hoppen, 'made a wider politicisation, possible'.[594] Hay was an essential part of that political process. He was part of the emerging Catholic nation and his work as secretary helped to create the environment where the masses were receptive to political ideas. O'Connell has been praised for 'harnessing the masses'.[595] Yet, Hay's incessant efforts, behind the scenes, to keep Catholics informed about the work of the Catholic body ensured that they were, to extend the equine metaphor, curried, groomed and ready to be harnessed by O'Connell. Like his contemporary William Drennan, Hay was 'a stable unseen power'.[596] Hay may have been unseen but he was certainly noticed by contemporaries.

Hay's 'zeal' and 'fluency in letter writing' provoked John Philpott Curran, the controversial barrister, to declare, 'he was a learned pig, who would run you down at any distance, and grunt you to death with the weight of his correspondence'.[597] There is no doubting his talkativeness. Grattan described him as 'a well meaning person; very busy, always in a bustle, and extremely loquacious … [as well as] active, honest and ardent'.[598] Hay's old friend Fingall asserted that it was 'impossible to do justice to his indefatigable zeal and exertions'.[599] The well-known writer and publisher W.J. Fitzpatrick maintained that Hay was 'a fussy, smart, and, at times, an indiscreet man, but one must hope "honest"'. This reference to Hay's honesty was a reaction to O'Connell's ironic description of Hay as 'honest Ned'.[600]

Hay's contemporaries agreed that he had exerted himself on behalf of the Catholics. Ultimately, as O'Connell pointed out, he 'succeeded for his country but failed for himself'.[601] Edward Hay was one of the creators of nineteenth-century Ireland.

ENDNOTES

1   For a comparable figure, see detailed
    work of Brian MacDermot (ed.),
    *The Catholic Question in England and
    Ireland: The Papers of Denys Scully 1798-
    1822* (Dublin, 1988), hereafter *Scully
    papers*. Denys Scully (1773-1830) and
    Hay were contemporaries. They both
    worked behind the scenes on behalf
    of Catholic emancipation. Scully's
    career as 'a barrister and politi-
    cal activist' is summarised in Brian
    MacDermot's entry in H.C.G. Mat-
    thew & Brian Harrison (eds), *Oxford
    Dictionary of National Biography, Vol. 49*
    (Oxford, 2004), p. 583.

2   He received an entry in S.J. Con-
    nolly (ed.), *The Oxford Companion
    to Irish History* (Oxford, 1998), p. 236.
    Hay featured in the old *Dictionary
    of National Biography*, this entry was
    written by the Dublin bibliophile
    J.T. Gilbert; it has been revised by
    Margaret Ó hÓgartaigh in the
    H.C.G. Matthew & Brian Harrison
    (eds), *Oxford Dictionary of National
    Biography Vol. 25* (Oxford, 2004),
    pp991-2. Hay's life is summarised
    in the *Dictionary of Irish Biography*
    (Cambridge, 2009).

3   Kevin Whelan, *The Tree of Lib-
    erty. Radicalism, Catholicism and the
    Construction of Irish Identity, 1760-1830*
    (Cork, 1996); L.M. Cullen, 'The 1798
    Rebellion in Wexford: United Irish-
    man Organisation, Membership and

    Leadership' in Kevin Whelan (ed.),
    Wexford: History and Society (Dublin,
    1987), pp222-247.

4   Daniel Gahan, *The People's Rising.
    The Wexford Rebellion of 1798* (Dublin,
    1995), p. 99.

5   Tom Dunne, *Rebellions. Memoir,
    Memory and 1798* (Dublin, 2004),
    especially pp102-104, 106, 111, 139,
    179-80, 182, 186, 195, 207, 217, 218,
    229-30, 247, 260 and 263.

6   Whelan, *The Tree of Liberty*, pp133-175.

7   Thomas Bartlett, David Dickson,
    Dáire Keogh & Kevin Whelan (eds),
    1798, A Bicentenary Perspective (Dub-
    lin, 2003), see, in particular, pp109,
    135, 450, 476, 483 and 609.

8   There are many biographies of
    O'Connell, for an elegant and
    incisive assessment of the most im-
    portant political figure in nine-
    teenth-century Ireland, see Oliver
    MacDonagh, *O'Connell: The Life of
    Daniel O'Connell, 1775-1847* (London,
    1991); Patrick Geoghegan's *King
    Dan. The Rise of Daniel O'Connell,
    1775-1829* (Dublin, 2008) refers to
    Hay's role in O'Connell's early
    career, see pp115,116, 173 and 175.

9   M.R. O'Connell (ed.), *The Cor-
    respondence of Daniel O'Connell 8
    Vols* (Shannon, 1972-81), hereafter
    O'Connell correspondence.

10 Dublin Diocesan Archives, Catholic
    Association Papers (hereafter DDA

CAP), 54/1, 54/2, 55/3, 60/2, 390/1 and 390/2. For a useful summary of these papers see Fergus O'Higgins, 'Catholic Association Papers in the Dublin Diocesan Archives' in *Archivium Hibernicum* 36, 1984, pp58-61.

[11] *Scully papers*.

[12] V.J. McNally, 'Archbishop Troy and the Catholic Church in Ireland, 1787-1817' (PhD, TCD, 1977), now published as *Reform, revolution and reaction; Archbishop John Thomas Troy and the Catholic Church in Ireland 1787-1817* (London, 1995); Dáire Keogh, '"The pattern of the flock": John Thomas Troy, 1786-1823' in James Kelly & Dáire Keogh (eds), *History of the Catholic Diocese of Dublin* (Dublin, 2000), pp215-236.

[13] Thomas Bartlett, *The Fall and Rise of the Irish Nation. The Catholic Question in Ireland, 1690-1830* (Dublin, 1992).

[14] Eamon O'Flaherty, 'The Catholic Convention and Anglo-Irish Politics, 1791-3' in *Archivium Hibernicum* 40, 1985, pp14-34.

[15] C.C. Woods & R.E. Ward (eds), *The Letters of Charles O'Conor of Belanagare 2 Vols* (Ann Arbor, 1980).

[16] Maureen McGeehin, 'The Activities and Personnel of the General Committee of the Catholic of Ireland 1767-1784' (MA, UCD, 1952), p.xi.

[17] P.J. Corish, *The Catholic Community in the Seventeenth and Eighteenth Centuries* (Dublin, 1981), p.219; R.F. Foster, 'Ascendancy and Union' in R.F. Foster (ed.), *The Oxford Illustrated History of Ireland* (Oxford, 1989), pp161-221, p.180.

[18] O'Flaherty, 'The Catholic Convention', p.15.

[19] Maureen Wall, 'The Whiteboys' in T. Desmond Williams (ed.), *Secret Societies in Ireland* (Dublin, 1973), pp13-25, p.14.

[20] Wall, 'The Whiteboys'.

[21] James Kelly, 'The Parliamentary Reform Movement of the 1790s and the Catholic Question' in *Archivium Hibernicum* 42, 1988, pp95-117, p.101.

[22] *Ibid.*, p.96.

[23] Edward Hay, *History of the Insurrection of County Wexford AD 1798* (Dublin, 1803), p.13.

[24] Cited in Kevin Whelan, 'Politicisation in County Wexford and the Origins of the 1798 Rebellion' in Hugh Gough & David Dickson (eds), *Ireland and the French Revolution* (Dublin, 1990), pp156-178, p.159.

[25] P.D. Smyth, 'The Volunteers and Parliament' in Thomas Bartlett & David Hayton (eds), *Penal Era and Golden Age* (Belfast, 1979), pp113-136, p.125.

[26] Marianne Elliott, *Wolfe Tone. Prophet of Irish Independence* (New Haven and London, 1989), pp113-115.

[27] Elliott, *Wolfe Tone*, p.131.

[28] L.M. Cullen, 'The Dublin Merchant Community in the Eighteenth Century' in Paul Butel & L.M. Cullen (eds), *French and Irish Perspectives on Urban Development, 1500-1900* (Dublin 1988), pp95-209.

[29] Kevin Whelan, 'The Catholic Community in Eighteenth Century County Wexford' in Kevin Whelan & T.P. Power (eds), *Endurance and Emergence. Catholic in Eighteenth-Century Ireland* (Dublin, 1990), p.152; Kevin Whelan, 'The Catholic Parish, the Catholic Chapel and Village Development in Ireland' in *Irish Geography* 1983, pp1-15.

[30] Kevin Whelan, 'The Catholic Church in County Tipperary, 1700-1900' in William Nolan (ed.) & T.G. McGrath (associate ed.), *Tipperary: History and Society* (Dublin, 1985), pp215-255, pp216-219.

[31] Eamon Duffy, 'Ecclesiastical Democracy Detected: 1 (1779-1787)' in *Recusant History* 10, 4, Jan. 1970, pp193-209.

[32] Robert Lynd, cited in untitled newspaper cutting, *c.*1916, in Barton

Ms 5637, NLI. The Barton family home in Wicklow had been overrun with rebels in the Rebellion of 1798. The Bartons were later associated with national movements in the late nineteenth and early twentieth centuries. Robert Barton signed the Anglo-Irish Treaty in 1921.

33 For an original analysis of the interactions between land ownership and politics in Wexford, see Daniel Gahan, 'Class, religion and rebellion: Wexford in 1798' in Jim Smyth (ed.), *Revolution, counter-revolution and union* (Cambridge, 2000), pp82-98.

34 Kevin Whelan, 'Catholic Mobilisa-tion, 1750-1850' in Paul Bergeron & L.M. Cullen (eds), *Culture et Pratiques Politiques en France et en Irlande XVIe-XVIIIe* (Paris, 1991), pp235-258, p.235; Whelan, 'The Catholic Parish', p.13.

35 Whelan, 'Politicisation in County Wexford', p.157.

36 Philip Hore, *History of the Town of Wexford Vol.IV* (London, 1900-1906), p.482.

37 Hilary Murphy, *Families of Wexford* (Wexford, 1986), p.121.

38 For Madden's career, see C.J. Woods, 'R.R. Madden, historian of the United Irishmen' in Bartlett, Dick-son, Keogh & Whelan (eds), *1798*, pp497-511.

39 Edmund Hogan, *The Description of Ireland and the State thereof as it is at this time present in Anno.1598* (Dublin, 1879), pp59-60.

40 Nicholas Furlong & John Hayes, *County Wexford in the Rare Oul' Times Vol.II* (Wexford, 1987), p.145.

41 J.H. O'Hart, *The Irish and Anglo-Irish Landed Gentry* (Shannon, 1969).

42 Hilary Murphy, *Wexford Families*, p.122; Patrick Corish, 'Two centuries of Catholicism in County Wexford' in Whelan (ed.), *Wexford: History and Society*, pp222-247, p.243.

43 R.R. Madden, *The Lives of the United Irishmen Vol.IV 4th series* (Dublin, 1860), p.531, all future references to Madden's work are from this volume and series; Hilary Murphy, *Wexford Families*, p.123.

44 Watty Cox's, *Irish Magazine* August 1808, p.367.

45 R.R. Madden, *United Irishmen*, p.53; Betham, *Prerogative Marriage Abstracts Series IV Vol.8*, 1753-1800.

46 Richard Musgrave, *Memoirs of the Different Rebellions in Ireland* (Dublin, 1801), p.44. For a perceptive analysis of Musgrave's career, see David Dickson, 'Foreword' in Steven W. Myers & Dolores E. McKnight (eds), *Memoirs of the Different Rebellions in Ireland, by Sir Richard Musgrave, Bart.* (Fort Wayne, 1995), ppi-xiii.

47 Hay to Lord Cornwallis, 19 July 1799, Royal Irish Academy, Bur-rowes Ms 23 K53.

48 This phenomenon of only men-tioning males has not disappeared amongst historians of the United Irishmen. In 1998-9, the Women's History Project published the Wil-liam Drennan and Martha McTier correspondence which was edited by Jean Agnew. The general editor was Maria Luddy. However, in 2000 this was described as 'a new 3 vol-ume edition of the correspondence of the Presbyterian radical William Drennan'. Martha McTier does not count! See Thomas Bartlett, 'Why the history of the 1798 Rebellion has yet to be written', *Eighteenth-Century Ireland* Vol. 15, 2000, p.181. Kevin Whelan suggested that Martha McTier's 'pragmatic political intelli-gence' was more impressive than that of her famous brother, see Bartlett, Dickson, Keogh & Whelan (eds), *1798*, p.470.

49 W.H. Jeffrey, *Castles of Wexford* (Wex-ford, 1979), p.18; Correspondence of

the Hay family courtesy of William
Sweetman, Wexford.

50 Information courtesy of the Maher
family, Ballinkeele House, County
Wexford.

51 For example Patricius Hay of
Wexford was a student in the Irish
College at Salamanca in the early
seventeenth century, 'Students of the
Irish College Salamanca (1595-1619)'
in *Archivium Hibernicum* 2, 1913, p.29.

52 Madden, *United Irishmen* p.533; Jeffrey, *Castles of Wexford*, p.181.

53 Peter Birch, *St Kieran's College
Kilkenny* (Dublin, 1951), p.29.
According to the archives at the
school, both Philip and James were
students there, see Dowling papers,
St Kieran's College, Kilkenny. It
was all too common for soldiers to
perish in the West Indies, 'at least
50,000' died there between 1793 and
1802, William Hague, *William Pitt the
Younger* (London, 2005), p.400.

54 *Dictionary of National Biography*; Hay
History, p.iii.

55 Watty Cox's, *Irish Magazine* Aug
1808, p.368. If this article was written by Hay, and the information
contained therein suggests that it is,
then it was all the more important in
ascertaining Hay's self-perception.

56 Hay to Cardinal Litta (Rome), 15 Aug.
1817, published in *Dublin Evening Post*
(hereafter *DEP*), 26 Jan. 1822.

57 Kevin Whelan, 'The Catholic Community in Eighteenth-Century
County Wexford' in Power & Whelan (eds), *Endurance and Emergence*,
pp129-170, p.155.

58 Whelan, 'Catholic Community in
Eighteenth-Century County Wexford', p.156.

59 Kevin Whelan (ed.), *A History of
Newbawn* (Newbawn, 1986), pp56-
64; John Mannion, 'A Transatlantic
Merchant Fishery: Richard Welsh
of New Ross and the Sweetmans of

Newfoundland 1734-1862' in Whelan (ed.), *Wexford: History and Society*,
pp373-421, especially pp381-405. According to some correspondence of
the Hay family (courtesy of William
Sweetman, Wexford) the Hays and
the Sweetmans were related.

60 Mannion, 'Transatlantic Merchant
Fishery', p.383.

61 Whelan, 'Catholic Mobilisation', p.236.

62 Whelan, 'Catholic Mobilisation', p.252.

63 Hay, *History*, *passim*.

64 Whelan, 'The Catholic Parish', pp1-15.

65 Maureen Wall, 'The Rise of a Catholic Middle Class in Eighteenth-Century Ireland' in *Irish Historical Studies*
(hereafter *IHS*), 11, 42, 1958, pp91-115.

66 Whelan, 'Politicisation in County
Wexford', p.172.

67 Eamon O'Flaherty, 'Irish Catholics and the French Revolution' in
Gough & Dickson (eds) *Ireland and
the French Revolution*, pp52-67, p.61.

68 R.B. McDowell, *Ireland in the Age of
Imperialism and Revolution* (Oxford,
1979), p.400.

69 Eamon O'Flaherty, 'The Catholic
Question in Ireland 1774-1793' (MA,
UCD, 1981), p.139.

70 Cited in Whelan, 'Politicisation in
County Wexford', p.168.

71 Marianne Elliott, 'Wolfe Tone and
the Development of a Revolutionary Culture in Ireland' in Bergeron
& Cullen (eds), *Culture et Pratique
Politiques*, pp171-186, p.182.

72 E.M. Johnston, 'Problems Common
to both Protestant and Catholic
Churches in Eighteenth Century
Ireland' in Oliver MacDonagh, W.F.
Mandle & Pauric Travers (eds), *Irish
Culture and Nationalism, 1750-1950*
(London, 1983), pp14-39, p.34.

73 William Drennan describing Tone, 5
July 1791, cited in Elliott, *Wolfe Tone*,
p.125.

74 McDowell, *Imperialism and Revolution*,
p.405.

75 Eamon O'Flaherty, 'The Catholic Convention and Anglo-Irish Politics' in *Archivium Hibernicum* 40 1985, pp14-34, p.26. For details on all those who attended the Catholic Convention, see C.J.Woods, 'The personnel of the Catholic Convention, 1792-3' in *Archivium Hibernicum* 57, 2003, pp26-76.

76 For a prosopographical analysis of the Catholic Convention, see C.J. Woods, 'The social composition of the Catholic Convention, 1792-3' in David Dickson & Cormac Ó Gráda (eds), *Refiguring Ireland. Essays in Honour of L.M. Cullen* (Dublin, 2003), pp165-171.

77 Elliott, 'Wolfe Tone and the Development of a Revolutionary Culture in Ireland', p.182.

78 James Smyth, 'Popular Politicisation in Ireland in the 1790s' (PhD, Cambridge, 1989), p.181.

79 Lord Donoughmore to Francis Hely-Hutchinson, 2 Nov. 1792, *Historical Manuscripts Commission* (Donoughmore) 12th Report, Appendix IX, p.324.

80 Henry Grattan (Jr), *Memoirs of the Right Honourable Henry Grattan Vol.V* (London, 1849), p.53.

81 D.G. Boyce, *Nineteenth Century: The Search for Stability: New Gill History of Ireland Vol.V* (Dublin, 1990), p.15.

82 Whelan, 'Catholic Mobilisation', p.255.

83 Hay to Grattan, 6 July 1802, Appendix No.VIII in J.B. Gordon, *History of the Rebellion in the Year 1798* 2nd ed. (Dublin, 1803), p.430. Hay unconvincingly denied that there was any connection between the United Irishmen and the Catholic Committee, p.431.

84 O'Flaherty, 'The Catholic Convention', p.12.

85 L.M. Cullen, 'The 1798 Rebellion in its Eighteenth-Century Context' in P.J. Corish (ed.), *Radicals, Rebels and Establishment: Historical Studies XV* (Belfast, 1985), pp91-113, p.103.

86 O'Flaherty, 'The Catholic Convention', p.176

87 See Hay's correspondence in DDA CAP 309/1.

88 Dáire Keogh, *'The French Disease': the Catholic Church and Radicalism in Ireland, 1790-1800* (Dublin, 1993).

89 O'Flaherty, 'The Catholic Convention', p.107.

90 Kevin Whelan, 'Catholics, Politicisation and the 1798 Rebellion' in Reamonn Ó Muirí (ed.), *Irish Church History Today* (Armagh, 1991), pp63-83, p.69.

91 McDowell, *Imperialism and Revolution*, p.418.

92 Cited in McDowell, *Imperialism and Revolution*, p.420.

93 Foster to Sheffield, 1 Aug. 1793, Public Record Office of Northern Ireland [hereafter PRONI] T.2965/103 in A.P.W. Malcomson, *An Anglo-Irish Dialogue. A Calendar of the Correspondence between John Foster and Lord Sheffield 1774-1821* (Belfast, 1975).

94 For example, Hay wrote that the recall of Fitzwilliam 'dashed the cup of expectations from our lips', Hay to Litta 15 Aug. 1817 in *DEP* 26 Jan. 1822.

95 Thomas Bartlett, '"A weapon of war, yet untried": Irish Catholics and the armed forces of the crown' in T.J. Fraser & Keith Jeffery (eds), *Men, Women and War: Historical Studies XVIII* (Dublin, 1993), pp66-85.

96 Cullen, 'The 1798 Rebellion in its Eighteenth-Century Context', p.102.

97 Thomas Bartlett, 'An End to Moral Economy. The Irish Militia Disturbances of 1798' in *Past and Present* 99, 1983, pp41-64, p.52; Thomas Powell, 'The Background to the Rebellion in County Wexford, 1790-98 (MA, UCD, 1970), p.76.

98 Certificate of Solomon Richards, Appendix No.III, reproduced in

Edward Hay, *History of the Insurrection of the County of Wexford AD 1798* (Dublin, 1898), p.315.

99 Hay, *History* (New York, 1873), pp25-30.

100 Bartlett, 'Militia Disturbances', p.52.

101 Hay, *History* (New York, 1873), p.30, 35.

102 Ivan Nelson, '"The first chapter of 1798?" Restoring a military perspective to the Irish Militia riots of 1793' in *IHS*, 33, 132, November 2003, pp369-386, p.386.

103 *DEP*, 18 May 1793.

104 Powell, 'Background to 1798', p.73.

105 Hore, *History of Wexford*, p.170.

106 Madden, *Lives of the United Irishmen*, p.524.

107 Whelan, 'Catholics, Politicisation and the 1798 Rebellion', p.78.

108 Whelan, 'Politicisation in County Wexford', p.169.

109 Caulfield to Troy, 22 Apr. 1792, DDA Troy Correspondence, cited in O'Flaherty, 'The Catholic Convention', p.141.

110 Thomas Bartlett, 'Select Documents XXXVIII: Defenders and Defenderism in 1795' in *IHS*, 24, 95, May 1985, pp372-294.

111 Bartlett, 'Defenders and Defenderism', p.365.

112 Hay, *History* (New York, 1873), p.vi.

113 Hay's involvement in various political activities is summarised in Kevin Whelan, 'Interpreting the 1798 Rebellion in County Wexford' in Dáire Keogh & Nicholas Furlong (eds), *The Mighty Wave. The 1798 Rebellion in Wexford* (Dublin, 1996), pp9-36, p.14.

114 John Thomas Troy to Edward Wakefield, 5 April 1811, cited in Edward Wakefield, *An Account of Ireland, Statistical and Political Vol. II* (London, 1812), p.592; cited in Whelan, *Tree of Liberty*, p.90, 195.

115 Hay to a Roman Catholic Bishop, copy of a proposed circular, 8 Sept. 1795, in Pelham Transcripts PRONI T755(2); Hay's census is located in the Fitzwilliam Papers in Sheffield Library, Yorkshire and a sample form of the census is in the Appendix of the National Library of Ireland copy of his *History* (Dublin, 1803).

116 Camden to Pelham, 26 Sept. 1795, in Pelham Transcripts PRONI T.755(2).

117 Edward Cooke to Pelham, 4 Dec. 1795, in Pelham Transcripts PRONI T.755(2).

118 Thomas Bartlett, 'Protestant nationalism in eighteenth-century Ireland' in Michael O'Dea & Kevin O'Dea (eds), *Nations and Nationalisms: France, Britain and Ireland in the eighteenth-century context* (Oxford, 1995), pp79-88, p.85.

119 Musgrave to Thomas Percy, Bishop of Dromore, 28 Jan. 1799, NLI Ms 4157, f.7.

120 William Todd Jones, *A Letter to the Societies of United Irishmen of the town of Belfast* (Dublin, 1792).

121 Edward Hay to Edmund Burke, 21 Jun. 1795, in R.B. McDowell (ed.), *Correspondence of Edmund Burke 1794-96 Vol. VIII* (Chicago, 1969), p.270.

122 Hay circular to a Roman Bishop, copy of a proposed circular, 8 Sept. 1975, in Pelham Transcripts PRONI T.755(2).

123 G.P. Bushe, 'An Essay towards ascertaining the population of Ireland' in *Transactions of the Royal Irish Academy, Vol. III*, 1789-90, pp145-55.

124 David Dickson, Cormac Ó Gráda & Stuart Daultrey, 'Hearth Tax, Household Size and Irish Population Change 1672-1821' in *Proceedings of the Royal Irish Academy*, 82c, 1982, pp125-81, p.147.

125 Hay to Cardinal Litta, 15 Aug. 1817, published in *DEP*, 26 Jan. 1822.

126 Thomas Newenham, *A Statistical and Historical Inquiry into the Progress and*

Magnitude of the Population of Ireland (London, 1805); Hay to Litta, 15 Aug. 1817, in *DEP*, 26 Jan. 1822. According to J.J. Lee, Newenham, who was very accurate in his calculations, 'made effective use of scattered *ad hoc* parochial returns'. J.J. Lee, *The Population of Ireland before the 19th Century* (London, 1973). Hence, Hay's census is of some use to demographic historians.

127 Hay, *History* (New York, 1973), p.ix.

128 Hay to Luke Teeling, 8 Sept. 1795, in NLI Reports on Private Collections no.261.

129 Burke to Hussey, 9 Jun. 1795, Fitzwilliam Papers NLI p 5641 and 5643.

130 Fitzwilliam to Burke, 2 Jun. 1795 in Fitzwilliam Papers NLI p 5641 and 5643.

131 Burke to Hay, 26 Jun. 1795, in Fitzwilliam Papers NLI p 5641 and 5643.

132 Hay to Teeling, 30 Sept. 1795, in *Reports on Private Collections* no.261.

133 Cooke to Pelham, 1795, Pelham Transcripts PRONI T.755.

134 Bartlett, *Fall and Rise of the Irish Nation*, p.206.

135 Foster to Sheffield, 23 May 1795, PRONI T.2965/114 in *Anglo-Irish Dialogue*.

136 Musgrave to Portland, 6 Jun. 1795, PRONI T.2905/4/39 in *Anglo-Irish Dialogue*.

137 Cullen, 'The 1798 Rebellion in its Eighteenth-Century Context', p.111.

138 Hay to Fitzwilliam, 21 Jun. 1795, in Fitzwilliam Papers NLI. p.5641 and 5643; Hay, *History* (New York, 1873), p.37; Hay to Litta, 15 Aug. 1817, in *DEP*, 26 Jan. 1822.

139 Hay to *DEP*, 18 Dec. 1819.

140 Cullen, 'The 1798 Rebellion in its Eighteenth-Century Context', p.104.

141 Whelan, 'The Religious Factor in 1798', p.66; Hay, *History* (New York, 1873), Appendix vi, p.xviii.

142 Hay, *History* (Dublin, 1898), Appendix vi, p.237.

143 Whelan, 'Politicisation in County Wexford', p.158.

144 John Colclough to Caesar Colclough, 15 Sept. 1795, McPeake Papers PRONI T./3048/C/18.

145 Hay to Wexford Committee, 9 Aug. 1798, National Archives of Ireland, Rebellion Papers (hereafter NAI RP) 620/39/7.

146 Hay, *History* (Dublin, 1898), p.316.

147 Birch, *Kilkenny College,* p.30.

148 Madden, *United Irishmen*, p.536. For Fitzgerald's career, see Ruán O'Donnell, 'Edward Fitzgerald of Newpark' in *Journal of the Wexford Historical Society* 1998-99, 17, pp121-143.

149 'Case of Captain Philip Hay, 1798: A Narrative of the Proceedings of the Commissioners of Suffering Loyalists in the Case of Captain Philip Hay, of the 18th Light Dragoons, with Remarks thereon by George, Earl of Kingston' in *Cork Historical and Archaeological Society Journal* 10, 1904, pp190-204, p.194. I am grateful to Catherine O'Rourke, formerly county librarian, Wexford County Library, who provided me with a copy of this pamphlet in 1991.

150 Charles Dickson, *The Wexford Rising, Its Causes and its Course* (Tralee, 1955), Appendix xii, p.263.

151 Correspondence of the Hay family, courtesy of Bill Sweetman, Wexford.

152 Cited in Thomas Powell, 'An Economic Factor in the Wexford Rebellion of 1798' in *Studia Hibernica* 16, 1976, pp140-157, p.141.

153 Whelan, 'Politicisation in County Wexford', p.158; Cullen, 'The 1798 in its Eighteenth-Century Context'. p.105.

154 *Ibid.*; Hay, *History* (Dublin, 1803), p.53.

155 Hay, *History* (New York, 1873), p.xxxvii.

156 Hay *Ibid*, p.23, 41.

157 A Wexford Freeholder, *Observations on Edward Hay's History* (n.d.);

Whelan, 'Politicisation in County Wexford', p.162.

158 I am indebted to Kevin Whelan for information on Hay's census.

159 Patrick O'Donoghue, 'The Catholic Church in an Age of Revolution and Rebellion, 1782–1803' (PhD, UCD, 1975), p.332.

160 Edward Hay's grandfather was Edward Hay; his three eldest grandsons were all named after their grandfather, hence there are at least three Edward Hays in Wexford in the 1790s. They were first cousins. My thanks to Bill Sweetman, a direct descendant of Hay the historian's first cousin, for this information.

161 Tithe notice in papers of Christopher Taylor, Printer, Wexford, NLI Prints and Drawings. My thanks to Colette O'Daly for alerting me to the valuable Taylor papers in the NLI. Most of the material printed by Taylor was for the militia and the yeomanry.

162 Hay, *History* (New York, 1873), p.55.

163 General Johnson cited in Major Wilson to Bentwick, Portland Papers PRONI T.2905/21/91 in A.P.W. Malcomson (ed.), *Eighteen Irish Official Papers of Great Britain Private Collections: Vol.I* (Belfast, 1973), hereafter *Private Collections Vol.I*, p.187.

164 Camden to Pitt, 26 March 1798, NLI Ms 886/261-5; Camden to Pitt, 7 April 1798, NLI Ms 886/269-71, cited in Gillian O'Brien, 'Camden and the move towards Union' in Dáire Keogh & Kevin Whelan (eds), *Acts of Union. The causes, contexts, and consequences of the Act of Union* (Dublin, 2001), pp106-125, p.121. For Camden's career, see Gillian O'Brien, 'Lord Camden in Ireland, 1795-8: A Study in Anglo-Irish Relations' (PhD, University of Liverpool, 2002).

165 For the military context see Thomas Bartlett, 'Defence, counter-insurgen-cy and rebellion: Ireland, 1793-1803' in Thomas Bartlett & Keith Jeffery (eds), *A Military History of Ireland* (Cambridge, 1996), pp247-294.

166 Powell, 'Background to 1798', *passim*.

167 Powell, 'Economic Factors in 1798', p.145

168 (An army officer), 'A few observations on Mr Hay's exaggerated account of the insurrection in Wexford' (1833) Ms in NLI Joly copy of Hay, *History* (Dublin 1803); Whelan, 'Politicisation in County Wexford', pp171-172.

169 L.M. Cullen, 'Late Eighteenth-Century Politicisation in Ireland: Problems in its Study and its French Links' in Bergeron & Cullen (eds), *Culture et Pratique Politiques*, pp137-157, p.155.

170 L.M. Cullen, *The Emergence of Modern Ireland* (London, 1981), p.214. For an excellent narrative of the rebellion in Wexford see Gahan, *People's Rising*.

171 Hay to Cornwallis, 19 Jul. 1799, in RIA Burrowes Ms 23 K53.

172 Thomas Handcock, 'Narrative of the Battle of Enniscorthy on 28 May 1798' in NLI Ms 16,232, p[photostat] 37.

173 John Brownrigg, 'Letter on 1798', NLI Ms 27/485(3), p.7.

174 Caulfield to Troy, 31 Jul. 1798, DDA, Troy correspondence.

175 Testimony of Solomon Richards, 30 Aug. 1799, in NAI Frazer Ms No.3; Hay, *History* (Dublin, 1898); Testimony of Solomon Richards, 30 Aug. 1799, p.318; Testimony of Martha Richards, 30 Aug. 1799, p.319.

176 Cited in Madden, *United Irishmen*, p.535

177 Dickson, *The Wexford Rising*, p.218

178 Letters sent by Musgrave to Dublin Castle, 15 May 1803, Hay to Matt Sutton, 11 Jun. 1798, in RP NAI 620/66/44.

179 Hay, *History* (Dublin, 1803), Appendix xi, p.xxvii.

180 Francis Plowden, *An Historical Review of the State of Ireland from the Invasion of that Country under Henry II to its Union with Great Britain Vol.II* (London, 1803), p.742. Troy has been 'a principal patron of Mr Plowden's work, as he was of that abominable, traitorous libel, Hay's history of the rebellion in Wexford'. Redesdale to Perceval, 23 Oct. 1803, in A.P.W. Malcomson (ed.), *Eighteenth Century Irish Official Papers in Great Britain. Private Collections Vol.II* (Belfast, 1990), p.387.

181 Thomas Pakenham, *The Year of Liberty: The Great Irish Rebellion of 1798* (London, 1969), p.252. The erratic careers of Kingsborough and his family are discussed in Janet Todd, *Rebel Daughters: Ireland in conflict 1798* (London, 2003). Ironically, Kingsborough harassed the loyalist Philip Hay while supporting the rebel sympathiser Edward Hay. Kingsborough pursued an 'individual vendetta' against Philip. The latter challenged Kingsborough to a duel in 1804, see W.N. Osborough, 'Legal aspects of the 1798 rising, its suppression and the aftermath' in Bartlett, Dickson, Keogh & Whelan (eds), *1798*, pp437-468, p.462. Duelling seemed to be a Hay family pastime, as Edward was involved in at least two duels, one in 1802 and another in 1807. Perhaps the family had an exalted sense of their own honour. Alternatively, it may simply have been pugnacity. For details on Edward Hay's duels, see James Kelly, *'That Damn'd Thing Called Honour', Duelling in Ireland 1570-1860* (Cork, 1995), p.226 and Brenda Clifford, Brid Finnegan, Geraldine Gallagher & Mary Murphy, 'Duelling in early nineteenth-century Ireland' in *Retrospect: Journal of the Irish History Students' Association*, pp1-8.

182 Kingsborough quoted in Major R. Wilson to Lord William Bentinck, 4 Jul. 1798, in *Eighteenth-Century Irish Official Papers in Great Britain, Vol.I*, p.187, cited in Bartlett, *Fall and Rise*, p.240, 381.

183 *Faulkner's Dublin Journal* (hereafter *FDJ*), 31 May 1798; Richard Musgrave, *Memoirs of the Different Rebellions in Ireland* (Dublin, 1801), and George Taylor, *A History of the Rise, Progress, Cruelties and Suppression of the Rebellion of the County of Wexford in the year 1798* (Dublin, 1803).

184 Thomas Bartlett, 'Review of A New History of Ireland' in *Past and Present* no.116, 1987, pp206-219, p.217.

185 Hay, *History* (New York, 1873), p.121, 233.

186 For a perceptive analysis of Scullabogue, see Dunne, *Rebellions*, pp247-264. Drawing on Daniel Gahan's figures, Dunne calculated that there were 124 Scullabogue victims, 113 Protestants and 11 Catholics, pp255-257. Donnelly focused on the sectarianism in Hay's account and argued that Hay calculated that eighty were killed inside the barn and forty outside it, yet Hay's overall figure (120) was remarkably accurate. See James S. Donnelly Jr, 'Sectarianism in 1798 and in Catholic nationalist memory' in Lawrence M. Geary (ed.), *Rebellion and remembrance in modern Ireland* (Dublin, 2001), pp15-37, p.28.

187 Brownrigg, *Letter on 1798*, p.14.

188 P.F. Kavanagh, *A Popular History of the Insurrection* (Cork, 1898), p.215.

189 Hay, *History* (New York, 1873), p.94.

190 Dickson, *The Wexford Rising*, pp151-152.

191 Alicia Pounden, a member of a liberal, Protestant family, quoted from a document her family received in 1798, which mentioned the Republic. 'As this House and Demesne have been surrendered for the use of the Republic, it is requested, that no person will do any injury', cited

in John D. Beatty (ed.), *Protestant women's narratives of the Irish rebellion of 1798* (Dublin, 2001), p.151.

192 *FJ*, 30 Jun. 1798.

193 Testimonial of Solomon Richards, Aug. 1799, NAI Frazer Ms No.ii.

194 Gordon, *History of the Rebellion*, Appendix no.ii, p.433.

195 Hay, *History* (Dublin, 1803), p.xvii, xx.

196 For a photograph of the memorial erected at Kilmallock Graveyard, Wexford in 1938 in honour of John Hay, see Margaret Ó hÓgartaigh, 'Edward Hay, Wexford Historian of 1798' in *Journal of the Wexford Historical Society* no.17, 1998-99, pp159-175, p.172. My thanks to Celestine Murphy for her help with the photographs and graph in this article.

197 Testimonial of Edward Roche, 18 Apr. 1799 in *Cornwallis Correspondence Vol.II*, 2nd edition, p.372.

198 Peadar MacSuibhne, *'98 in Carlow* (Carlow, 1974), p.91.

199 P.F. Kavanagh, *A Popular History of the Insurrection of 1798* (Cork, 1898), p.264; Hay, *History* (Dublin, 1803), p.xx.

200 Gordon, *History*, Appendix no.viii, p.434.

201 Thomas Taylor (sworn before Eden Jacob) to Gordon, 28 Aug. 1799 in Gordon, *History*, p.435.

202 Michael Bourke to Hay, 3 Jun. 1799, in Gordon, *History*, p.438.

203 'Vortex' was the title given to the last chapter in David Dickson's seminal *New Foundations: Ireland 1660-1800* (Dublin, 2000, second revised and enlarged edition), p.189.

204 McDowell, *Ireland in the Age of Imperialism and Revolution*, p.677.

205 W.N. Osborough, 'Legal aspects of the 1798 Rising, its suppression and the aftermath' in Bartlett, Dickson, Keogh & Whelan (eds), *1798*, pp437-468, pp438-439.

206 Hay to Cornwallis, 19 Jul. 1799, in RIA Burrowes Ms 23 K53.

207 Hay to Earl Moira (enclosure for General Hunter), 20 Mar. 1800, NAI Frazer Ms no.iii.

208 Hay, *History* (Dublin, 1803), p.xxxiii.

209 John Colclough to Lady Catherine Colclough, 11 Dec. 1799, McPeake Papers PRONI T.3048/C.18.

210 Madden, *History of the United Irishmen*, p.536.

211 Trial of Philip Hay, 4 Jul. 1798 Sirr Papers, TCD Manuscripts Department, 896/6, ff 6-7.

212 'Case of Captain Philip Hay', pp194-197.

213 'Case of Captain Philip Hay', p.198. Kingsborough's life is excellently summarised in David Murphy's entry in James McGuire (ed.), *Dictionary of Irish Biography* (Cambridge, 2009). I am grateful to David Murphy for allowing me to see an advance copy of his article.

214 Lease courtesy of the Maher Family, Ballinkeele, County Wexford. I am grateful to the Maher family for permission to examine this lease.

215 Correspondence of the Hay family, courtesy of William Sweetman; Kevin Whelan, 'The Religious Factor in the 1798 Rebellion', p.81.

216 See Musgrave's *Memoirs* for the classic loyalist response to 1798.

217 Caulfield to Troy, 10 Sept. 1799, in Caulfield Troy Correspondence, DDA.

218 Caulfield to Troy, 3 Nov. 1799, in Caulfield Troy Correspondence, DDA.

219 Caulfield to Troy, 17 Dec. 1799, in Caulfield Troy Correspondence, DDA.

220 Hay, *History* (Dublin, 1803), p.xxxiii.

221 George Taylor, *A History of the Rise, Progress, Cruelties and Suppression of the Rebellion in the County of Wexford* (Dublin, 1800).

222 Musgrave, *Memoirs*, *passim*.

223 Dickson, *Wexford*, p.216.

224 Musgrave to Hardwicke, 15 Mar. 1803, NAI RP 620/66/74.

225 Hay, *History* (Dublin, 1803), p.3, 6, 14, 16.

226 Margaret Ó hÓgartaigh, 'Making History and Defining the Nation: Nineteenth-century interpretations of 1798' in Philip Bull, Frances Devlin-Glass & Helen Doyle (eds), *Ireland and Australia, 1798-1998. Studies in Culture, Identity and Migration* (Sydney, 2000), pp24-33, p.29.

227 Richard Musgrave to George Lenox-Conyngham, 27 Apr. 1799, PRONI, D1449/12/292, cited in Whelan, *The Tree of Liberty*, p.137, 201.

228 Musgrave Depositions, Manuscripts Department, Trinity College Dublin, Ms 871. These depositions provide revealing insights into the sense of terror felt by those caught in the line of fire during the rebellion.

229 Claire Connolly, 'Completing the Union? The Irish Novel and the Moment of Union' in Michael Brown, Patrick M. Geoghegan & James Kelly (eds), *The Irish Act of Union, 1800* (Dublin, 2003), pp157-175, p.164.

230 Ruán O'Donnell, *Robert Emmet and the Rising of 1803* (Dublin, 2003), p.42.

231 Gordon, *History* 2nd Edition (Dublin, 1803), Appendix no.viii.

232 Denise Kleinrichert, *Republican Internment and the Prison Ship* Argenta, *1922* (Dublin, 2001).

233 Fitzgerald to Hay, 19 May 1800, in Gordon, *History* 2nd Edition (Dublin, 1803), Appendix no.viii, p.445.

234 Kingston [Lord Kingsborough became the Earl of Kingston] to Hay, 14 Dec. 1799, in Gordon, *History* 2nd Edition (Dublin, 1803), Appendix no.viii, p.446.

235 Kingston to Hay, 14 Dec. 1799, in Gordon, *History* 2nd Edition (Dublin, 1803), Appendix no.viii, p.10.

236 Hay to Gordon, 6 Jul. 1802, in Gordon, *History* 2nd Edition (Dublin, 1803), Appendix no.viii, p.430.

237 Alexander Marsden to William Wickham, 9 Mar. 1803, PRONI, Wickham Ms T2627/5/K/166, cited in Whelan, *The Tree of Liberty*, p.160, 205.

238 Bartlett, *Fall and Rise*, p.319.

239 Hay, *History* (Dublin, 1803), p.i.

240 Hay, *History* (Dublin, 1803), ppiv-v.

241 Hay, *History* (Dublin, 1803), p.xii.

242 Hay, *History* (New York, 1873), p.159.

243 Hay, *History* (Dublin, 1803), p.xxviii.

244 Hay, *History* (Dublin, 1803), pp22-23.

245 Hay, *History* (Dublin, 1803), p.24, 46.

246 Hay, *History* (Dublin, 1803), p.50, 55.

247 Cullen, 'The 1798 Rebellion in Wexford: United Irish Organisation, Membership and Leadership', pp248-295.

248 Hay, *History* (Dublin, 1803), p.61.

249 Hay, *History* (Dublin, 1803), p.247. For further details on the Irish who defended various empires, from the British to the Hapsburg, see Harman Murtagh, 'Irish Soldiers Abroad, 1600-1800' in Bartlett & Jeffery (eds), *A Military History of Ireland*, pp294-314.

250 Hay, *History* (Dublin, 1803), p.80.

251 Hay, *History* (Dublin, 1803), p.88, 91.

252 Hay, *History* (Dublin, 1803), p.100.

253 Hay, *History* (New York, 1873), p.142.

254 Hay, *History* (Dublin, 1803), p.134.

255 Hay, *History* (Dublin, 1803), pp144-5.

256 Hay, *History* (Dublin, 1803), p.161; Cullen, 'Late Eighteenth-Century Politicisation in Ireland: Problems in its Study and its French Links', pp137-157, p.149.

257 Hay, *History* (Dublin, 1803), p.188.

258 Hay, *History* (Dublin, 1803), p.221.

259 Hay, *History* (Dublin, 1803), p.250.

260 Hay to Moira, 19 Feb. 1803, in NAI Fraser Ms no.iii; Hay to Moira, 10 Apr. 1803, in NAI Fraser Ms no.iii.

261 *DEP*, 10 Mar. 1803; *FDJ*, 17 March 1803.

262 *DEP*, 10 Mar. 1803.

263 *DEP*, 24 Mar. 1803. This price sug-

gests that Hay's book was aimed at an elite audience.

[264] Hay to Fitzwilliam, 10 Apr. 1803, Fraser Ms no. iii.

[265] *DEP*, 23 Apr. 1803.

[266] *DEP*, 28 Apr. and 3 May 1803.

[267] Fitzwilliam to Hay, 25 Sept. 1803, in NAI Fraser Ms no. iii; Grattan to Hay, 28 Dec. 1803 in NAI Fraser Ms no. iii.

[268] Morgan D'Arcy to Hay, 18 Apr. 1803, in NAI Fraser Ms no. iii; Daniel Delany to Hay, 8 Aug. 1803, in NAI Frazer Ms no. iii.

[269] This post is equivalent to Minister for Foreign Affairs at the Vatican.

[270] Hay to Litta, 15 Aug. 1817, in *DEP*, 26 Jan. 1822; Fox to Hay, 13 Jun. 1803, cited in *DEP*, 26 Jan. 1822.

[271] J.H. Andrews, 'Landmarks in Early Wexford Cartography' in Whelan, *Wexford*, pp447-466.

[272] Hay, *History* (Dublin, 1803); Hay, *History*, NLI Joly copy (Dublin, 1803); Hay, *History* (Dublin, 1842); Hay, *History* (Dublin, 1847); Hay, *History* published with Michael Doherty, *The History of the American Revolution* (Dublin, 1848); Hay, *History* (New York, 1873), and Hay, *History* (Dublin, 1898).

[273] Thomas Cloney, *A Personal Narrative of those Transactions in the County in which the Author was Engaged* (Dublin, 1832); Sean Cloney, 'The Cloney Families of County Wexford' in Whelan, *Wexford*, pp316-341; John Joyce, *General Thomas Cloney: Wexford Rebel of 1798* (Dublin, 1988).

[274] Cloney, *Personal Narrative*, p.19, 23, 247.

[275] Cloney to Hay (thirty-one letters) in DDA CAP 390/1/17.

[276] Cloney, *Personal Narrative*, p.63, 71.

[277] Hay, *History* (New York, 1873), pp235-236.

[278] Hay, *History* (New York, 1873), Appendix no. viii, p.431.

[279] C.H. Teeling, *History of the Irish Rebellion of 1798* (Shannon, 1972), p.256.

[280] George Taylor, *A History of the Rise, Progress, Cruelties and Suppression of the Rebellion of the County of Wexford in the Year 1798* (Belleville, 1864), p.155.

[281] Cornelius Grogan was executed during the rebellion.

[282] Jonah Barrington, *Rise and Fall of the Irish Nation* (Paris, 1833), p.36; Todd, *Rebel Daughters*, p.284.

[283] For an analysis of Byrne's career, see Thomas Bartlett, 'Miles Byrne: United Irishman, Irish Exile and Beau Sabreur' in Keogh & Furlong (eds), *The Mighty Wave*, pp118-138.

[284] Hay, *History* (New York, 1873), p.198.

[285] Miles Byrne, *Memoirs of Miles Byrne* (Shannon, 1972), pp185-186. The first edition was published in 1863.

[286] *Wolfe Tone Annual* 1948, series of articles devoted to 1798; Sinn Féin pamphlets in the NLI regularly included reading lists for their supporters. Hay does not feature on any of the lists but Byrne's and, not surprisingly, Wolfe Tone's works are frequently mentioned.

[287] Oliver Bond was a leading United Irishman in Dublin. His home was raided during a United Irish meeting, the United Irishmen were captured and valuable documentation was seized.

[288] Byrne, *Memoirs of Miles Byrne*, p.55, 181, 56.

[289] (An army officer) 'A few observations on Mr Hay's exaggerated account of the insurrection in Wexford' (n.d.), insert in NLI Joly copy of Hay, *History* (Dublin, 1803).

[290] Wexford Freeholder in Hay, *History* (Dublin, 1803), p.1, 5, 6.

[291] W.J. Fitzpatrick (ed.), *The correspondence of Daniel O'Connell Vol. II* (London, 1880), p.56.

[292] P.F. Kavanagh, *A Popular History of the Insurrection of 1798* (Cork, 1898), p.83.

[293] *Ibid.*, p.149.

[294] Anna Kinsella, '1798 Claimed for the Catholics: Father Kavanagh, Fenians and the Centenary Celebrations' in Keogh & Furlong (eds), *The Mighty Wave*, pp139-155.

[295] Kavanagh, *A Popular History of the Insurrection of 1798* (Cork, 1898), p.215.

[296] Hore, *History of Wexford*, p.405.

[297] Dickson, *Wexford Rising*, p.91, 151, 218.

[298] *Ibid.*, pp217-8.

[299] *Ibid.*, p.218.

[300] Thomas Pakenham, *The Year of Liberty: The Great Irish Rebellion of 1798* (London, 1969), p.247.

[301] Powell, *Background to the Rebellion*, p.67, ii.

[302] Jacqueline Hill, 'Popery and Protestantism, Civil and Religious Liberty: The Disputed Lessons of Irish History 1690-1812' in *Past and Present*, 118, 1988, pp96-129, p.128.

[303] Donal McCartney, 'Writings on Irish History in the Early Nineteenth Century: A Study in Irish Public Opinion 1800-1830' (MA, UCD, 1954), p.ix, 56.

[304] Thomas Dunne, ' Representations of Rebellion; 1798 in Literature; in F.B. Smith (ed.), *Ireland, England and Australia* (Canberra and Cork, 1990), pp14-40, p.17. Dunne's most impressive contribution to the historiography of 1798 is his *Rebellions*, where he described Hay's *History* as part of the 'main Catholic rebuttal of Musgrave', p.102.

[305] Thomas Dunne, 'Representations of Rebellion; 1798 in Literature', p.18.

[306] Ruan O'Donnell, 'General Holt and the Historians' in Bob Reece (ed.), *Irish Convicts: The Origins of Convicts Transported to America* (Dublin, 1989), p.31, 33.

[307] James Smyth, 'Popular Politicisation in Ireland in the 1790s' (PhD, Cambridge, 1989), p.178. This seminal thesis has now been published as *The men of no property: Irish radicals and popular politics in the late eighteenth century* (Dublin, 1992).

[308] Cullen, '1798 in its Eighteenth-Century Context', p.92.

[309] Cullen, 'Late Eighteenth-Century Politicisation in Ireland', p.147.

[310] *Ibid.*, p.149.

[311] Cullen, 'The 1798 Rebellion in Wexford: United Irish Organisation, Membership and Leadership', p.250-2.

[312] *Ibid.*, p.252.

[313] *Ibid.*, p.284

[314] Nicholas Furlong, *Fr Murphy of Boolavogue, 1753-1798* (Dublin, 1991), pp104-5.

[315] Cullen, 'The 1798 Rebellion in Wexford: United Irish Organisation, Membership and Leadership', pp293-294.

[316] Thomas Bartlett, 'Religious rivalries in France and Ireland in the age of the French Revolution' in *Eighteenth-Century Ireland, Iris an dá chultúr*, 6, 1991, pp57-76, p.67.

[317] Whelan, 'The Religious Factor in the 1798 Rebellion', p.82; Whelan's *Tree of Liberty* contains the most extensive discussion of Hay's *History*, pp156-160.

[318] Whelan, 'Catholics, Politicisation and the 1798 Rebellion', p.79.

[319] Hay, *History* (Dublin, 1842); Hay, *History* (Dublin, 1847); Hay, *History* published with Michael Doherty, *The History of the American Revolution* (Dublin, 1848). The 1847 edition of Hay's *History* advertised various publications of Duffy's Library of Ireland. These included *The Ballad Poetry of Ireland* by Charles Gavan Duffy, *The Poems of Thomas Davis* and John Mitchell's *The Life of Aodh O'Neill*. These texts reinforce the view that Hay's work was perceived as a nationalistic text. Hay's work

cost 1*s*, or one-fifth of its original price, thereby making it relatively affordable.

320 R.F. Foster, *Paddy and Mr Punch. Connections in Irish and English History* (London, 1993), p.5.

321 This edition was published by Kessingers in the United States in 1997.

322 P.F. Kavanagh, *A Popular History of the Insurrection of 1798* (Dublin, 1870), this is the first edition; Anna Kinsella, '1798 Claimed for Catholics: Father Kavanagh, Fenians and Centenary Celebrations', pp139-155.

323 James Kelly, 'Popular Politics in Ireland and the Act of Union' in *Transactions of the Royal Historical Society, Sixth Series, X* (Cambridge, 2000), pp259-287, p.261.

324 Catholic meetings Oct./Dec. 1804, Public Record Office, Home Office, Kew, now the UK National Archives [hereafter PRO HO] 123/19/109-46 and 16 Feb. 1805, PRO HO 30/81328/310. These important reports are available on microfilm in the NLI.

325 Denys Scully to Edward Hay, 24[?] Mar. 1805, in *Scully Papers* no.106A, p.98.

326 Denys Scully Diary, 6 Mar. 1805, NLI Ms 27, 514 (ii). This has now been edited by Brian MacDermot and published as *The Irish Catholic Petition of 1805: the diary of Denys Scully* (Dublin, 1992). Hay left his card at Scully's lodgings, p.73.

327 For Pitt and the Union see Patrick M. Geoghegan, *The Irish Act of Union* (Dublin, 1999) and his impressively concise *Lord Castlereagh* (Dundalk, 2002), p.39.

328 Redesdale [Lord Chancellor of Ireland] to Perceval, 25 Nov. 1804, PRONI T.3030/7/28 in *18th Century Private Collections Vol.II*, p.405.

329 DDA CAP Meeting on 28 Mar. 1806, 54/1/1/4. For Keogh's career,

see James Kelly's entry in the *Oxford DNB Vol. 31*, pp356-357; Aileen Donald, 'John Keogh: The Pursuit of Catholic Emancipation 1780-1795' (MA minor thesis, St Patrick's College, DCU, 1999), and Maureen Wall's brief, but incisive, essay in Gerard O'Brien (ed.) *Catholic Ireland in the Eighteenth Century – the Collected Essays of Maureen Wall* (Dublin, 1989).

330 Proceedings of the Catholic Committee, NLI Ms 27,530, pp194-195.

331 DDA CAP 54/1/1/2.

332 DDA CAP 10 Apr. 1806, 60/2/15/1.

333 Peter Jupp, *Lord Grenville 1759-1834* (Oxford, 1985), p.363.

334 This consisted of four elected representatives from each parish.

335 *DEP*, 3 May 1806. Hay was one of the presenters of the Wexford petition, *DEP*, 6 May 1806.

336 Catholic Meeting, 13 and 14 Mar. 1806, reported in *DEP*, 18 Mar 1806.

337 Fox to Hay, 20 Feb. 1806, British Library Additional Ms 47, 569/243. My thanks to Tom Bartlett for this reference.

338 Milner to Gibson (Bishop of Durham), 23 Feb. 1807, Durham University Catholic Archives, cited in McNally, 'Archbishop Troy', p.333.

339 Milner to Troy, 10 Feb. 1807, in Mc-Nally, 'Archbishop Troy', p.331.

340 Hay to Bedford, 5 Mar. 1807, *Historical Manuscripts Commission Report on the Manuscript of JB Fortescue Vol.9*, 1915, p.67.

341 Quoted in Peter Jupp, 'Dr Duigenan reconsidered' in Sabine Wichert (ed.), *From the United Irishmen to Twentieth-Century Unionism* (Dublin, 2004), pp79-96, p.82.

342 Bedford to Hay, 30 Aug. 1807, DDA CAP 390/1/14/3.

343 Hay's correspondence in DDA CAP 390/1, 24 files, 834 letters.

344 DDA CAP 54/1/2, Catholic Meetings 1807.

345 DDA CAP 54/1/2, Catholic Meetings 9 Feb. 1807 and 24 Feb. 1807.

346 DDA CAP 54/1/2, Catholic Meeting 24 Feb. 1807.

347 *DEP*, 18 July 1807; DDA CAP 54/1/2, Catholic Meeting 16 Feb. 1807.

348 For a summary see O'Higgins, 'Catholic Association Papers in the Dublin Diocesan Archives', pp 58-61.

349 Robert Meyler to Hay, 24 Jan. 1807; Henrietta Parsons to Hay, 9 Feb. 1807; Owen O'Conor to Hay, 16 Apr. 1807 in DDA CAP 390/1/1/2/6/8.

350 W.B. Caulfield to Hay, 3 Mar. 1807, DDA CAP 390/1/18/1.

351 Fingall to Hay, 14 Jan. and 18 Jan. 1807, DDA CAP 390/1/10/1/2.

352 Fingall to Hay, 23 Jan. and 24 Mar. 1807, DDA CAP 390/1/10/3/4.

353 Fingall to Hay, May 1807, DDA CAP 390/1/10/9.

354 P. McLaughlin to Hay, 4 Feb. 1807, DDA CAP 390/1/13/2.

355 John Milner to Hay, 18 Mar. 1807, DDA CAP 390/1/7/8.

356 5 Jan. 1808, unsigned report in PRO HO 100/147/13-14.

357 James Meyler to Hay, 15 Feb. 1808, DDA CAP 390/1/2/24.

358 Gerard O'Brien, 'The Beginning of the Veto Controversy in Ireland' in *Journal of Ecclesiastical History* 38, 1, 1987, pp 80-94, pp 84-85.

359 Litttedales to Beckett, 6[?] Aug. 1808, HO 100/148/190.

360 Kelly, *Duelling*, p.226.

361 S.J. Connolly, 'The Catholic Question, 1801-12' in W.E. Vaughan (ed.) *A New History of Ireland, Volume V: Ireland Under the Union I, 1801-1870* (Oxford, 1989), pp 24-47, pp 36-40.

362 *Scully Papers*, pp 184-5, 258.

363 H. Fitzpatrick to Hay (in London), 8 Jun. 1808, and J.K. Casey to Hay (in London), 19 Jun. 1808, in DDA CAP 390/1/2/54/55.

364 Connolly, 'The Catholic Question, 1801-12', p.41.

365 Watty Cox's *Irish Magazine* March 1815, pp 135-137; see also W.J. Fitzpatrick, *Lives, Letters and Correspondence of Dr Doyle (JKL) Bishop of Kildare and Leighlin Vol.I* (Dublin, 1880), p.40. Ryan was 'Haughty to everyone … and uniformly ungracious.'

366 Eamon Duffy, 'Ecclesiastical Democracy Detected: I (1779-1787)' in *Recusant History* 10, 4, 1970, pp 193-209.

367 Denys Scully to Charles Butler, 25 Aug. 1808 in *Scully Papers* no.181, pp 171-173.

368 Walter Redmond to Hay, 30 Jan., and James Bolger to Hay, 17 Feb. 1808, DDA CAP 390/1/2/10/17.

369 Revd James Barrett to Hay, 16 Jan. 1808, DDA CAP 390/1/2/3.

370 Hay from Bishops, 1808, DDA CAP 390/1/13/17/22/24/27.

371 P.J. Plunkett to Hay, 2 Feb. 1808, DDA CAP 390/113/29.

372 Dominic Bellew to Hay, 11 Apr. 1808, DDA CAP 390/1/13/37.

373 William Talbot to Hay, 9 Feb. 1808, DDA CAP 390/1/2/16.

374 Patrick Ryan to Hay, 6 Feb. 1808, DDA CAP 390/1/13/31.

375 Troy to Hay, 1808, DDA CAP 390/1/13/43.

376 Hay to R.B. Sheridan, no.specific date given, 1808, DDA CAP 390/1/19.

377 Michael Furlong to Thomas Cloney, 2 May 1810, DDACAP390/1/20/10.

378 Thomas Cloney to Hay, 12 Aug. 1808, DDA CAP 390/1/18/1; Philip Hay to Hay, 1 Nov. 1808, DDA CAP 390/118/6; Owen Sinnott to Hay, 10 Nov. 1808, DDA CAP 390/1/2/65.

379 Arthur Barker to Hay, 27 Dec. 1808, DDA CAP 390/1/2/66/67.

380 Minute Books of the Irish Catholic Committee I (May 1809-August 1810), II (August 1810-June 1811) NLI Ms 4321-4322, [hereafter Min-

ute Book I and II]; Minute Book I, 26 July 1809. All minutes of meetings were signed by Hay.

[381] Minute Book I, 22 Sept. 1809.

[382] Cloney to Hay, 28 July 1809, DDA CAP 390/1/17/l9.

[383] My thanks to Ruth McManus for pointing out that Capel Street was a significant commercial centre in early nineteenth-century Dublin.

[384] Minute Book I, 13 Nov. 1809.

[385] Minute Book I, 15 Nov. and 24 Nov. 1809.

[386] Catholic Meeting, 30 Nov. 1809, DDA CAP 54/1/5/31.

[387] Charles Butler to Hay, 19 May 1809, DDA CAP 390/1/2/3.

[388] Edward Jerningham to Hay, 26 May and 23 Jul., DDA CAP 390/1/15/2/4.

[389] Hay to Charles Butler, 12 Mar. 1809, DDA CAP 390/2/12/1.

[390] Hay to Edward Jerningham, 6 May 1809, DDA CAP 390/1/16/2.

[391] Charles Butler to Hay, 3 Jul. 1809, DDA CAP 390/2/12/6.

[392] The *DEP* on occasion produced a 'Catholic meeting supplement' in order to report on the most recent Catholic Committee meeting.

[393] For example, P.J. Plunkett of Kells was willing to 'do everything in' his power to help Hay. Troy sent Hay lists of constraints on the clergy for their 'Grievances Committee'. Bishops John Power of Waterford, James Murphy of Monaghan and Francis Reilly of Belturbet sent Hay a list of the parish priests in their dioceses; 5 Oct., 19 Nov., 13 Jun., 8 Jun. and 11 Jun. 1809, DDA CAP 390/1/13/50/54/46/44/45.

[394] Letters to Hay, 1809, DDA CAP 390/1/3.

[395] Edward Hay (Ross) to Hay, 7 August 1809, DDA CAP 390/1/18/15.

[396] Denys Scully to Richard Huddleston, 23 Jan. 1810 in *Scully Papers*

no.228, p.218.

[397] *DEP*, 10 Feb. 1810.

[398] *DEP*, 1 Feb. 1810.

[399] Hay to Daniel O'Connell, 28 Feb. 1810 in *O'Connell Correspondence I* no.271, pp214-215.

[400] Hay to Jerningham, 19 May 1810, DDA CAP 390/1/16/8.

[401] Hay to Edward Jerningham, 7 May 1810, DDA CAP 390/1/16/7.

[402] Catholic Meeting, 7 May 1810, DDA CAP 54/1/1/60.

[403] Daniel Delany to Daniel O'Connell, 19 May 1810 in *O'Connell Correspondence I*, no.282, p.221.

[404] Circular from O'Connell, 5 Jun. 1810, DDA CAP 54/1/5/63.

[405] Catholic Meeting, 25 Jan. 1810, DDA CAP 54/1/5/43.

[406] Edward Hay to Hay, 28 Jun. 1810, DDA CAP 390/1/18/25.

[407] Appendix No.1, Catholic Proceedings, DDA CAP 54/1, v, no.83.

[408] Pole to Ryder, 23 Jul. 1810, PRONI T. 3228/5/14 in *Private Collections Vol.II*, p.102.

[409] Bartlett, *Fall and Rise*, p.294.

[410] Catholic Circular, 1 Jan. 1811, DDA CAP 54/1/7/2.

[411] *DEP*, 19 Jan. 1811.

[412] *DEP*, 8 Jan. 1811 (the *DEP* did not specify what the report was about).

[413] DDA CAP 55/3/5/14, no date given.

[414] Draft of letter by Hay, 23 Feb. 1811, DDA CAP 390/19/21.

[415] Richmond to the Home Office, 6 Sept. 1811, HO 100/164/339 in *Scully Papers*, p.284.

[416] Troy to Hay, 10 Jan., and Young to Hay, 17 Oct. 1811, DDA CAP 390/1/13/70/77; Pádraig De Brún, 'The Irish Society's Bible Teachers, 1818-27', *Éigse, A Journal of Irish Studies*, xix, part II, 1983, pp281-332.

[417] Irene Hehir, 'New Lights and Old Enemies: The "Second Reformation" and the Catholics of Ireland, 1800-1835' (MA, University of Wisconsin,

1983). See David Hempton, 'Wesleyan Methodism and Educational Politics in Early Nineteenth-century England' in *History of Education*, Vol.8, No.3, 1979, pp207-221 for an analysis of similar activities in England.

[418] David Hempton, 'The Methodist Crusade in Ireland 1795-1845', *IHS* 22, 85, March 1980, pp33-48, p.37.

[419] Letters to Hay regarding the address and petition in 1811, DDA CAP 390/6.

[420] Donoughmore to Francis Hely-Hutchinson, 9 Feb. 1811 in Donoughmore Papers PRONI T.3459/F/10/54.

[421] *DEP*, 19 Mar. 1811.

[422] *DEP*, 2 Apr. 1811; *DEP*, 16 May 1811.

[423] Hay's circular to clergy, 28 Apr. 1811, DDA CAP 54/1/7/70.

[424] *DEP*, 18 Apr. 1811.

[425] *DEP*, 23 Apr. 1811

[426] Richmond to Ryder (Home Secretary), 28 Apr. 1811 in *Private Collections Vol.II*, p.86.

[427] *DEP*, 30 May 1811.

[428] *DEP*, 11 Jun. 1811.

[429] *DEP*, 14 Jun. 1811.

[430] See *Scully Papers*, p.358. An 'aggregate meeting is a public meeting, open to all', see Jacqueline Hill, 'Dublin After the Union: The Age of the Ultra Protestants, 1801-22' in Michael Brown, Patrick Geoghegan & James Kelly (eds), *The Irish Act of Union, 1800. Bicentennial Essays* (Dublin, 2003), pp144-56, fn 1, p.225.

[431] Donoughmore to Francis Hely Hutchinson, 9 Feb. 1811 in Donoughmore Papers, PRONI T.3459/F/10/54.

[432] For lay involvement in the Irish Church see D.A. Leighton, 'Gallicanism and the Veto Controversy: Church, State and Catholic Community in early Nineteenth Century Ireland' in Mary Cullen, Vincent Comerford, Jacqueline Hill & Colm Lennon (eds), *Religion, Conflict and Coexistence* (Dublin, 1989), pp135-158.

[433] Oliver MacDonagh, 'The Politicisation of Irish Catholic Bishops, 1800-1850' in *Historical Journal* 18, 1975, pp37-53, p.40.

[434] Hay to Jerningham, 11 Feb. and 2 Mar. 1811, DDA CAP 390/1/16/17/24.

[435] Milner to Scully, 16 Dec. 1812, in *Scully Papers*, p.258.

[436] William Poynter to Hay, 2 May 1811, DDA CAP 390/1/13/79.

[437] To Hay from various individuals, 1811, DDA CAP 390/1/5.

[438] Fingall to Hay, 4 Jan., 27 Jan. and 30 Aug. 1811, DDA CAP 390/1/51/63; Margaret Ó hÓgartaigh, 'Lord Fingall of Killeen Castle and Edward Hay of Wexford: Catholic Politics in the late eighteenth and early nineteeth century', *Ríocht na Midhe, Records of the Meath Archaeological and Historical Society*, Vol.xviii, 2007, pp151-155.

[439] Catholic Meeting, 20 Apr. 1811, DDA CAP 54/1/7/77.

[440] *DEP*, 14 May 1811.

[441] *DEP*, 30 Apr. 1811.

[442] *DEP*, 9 May 1811.

[443] *DEP*, 9 Jul. 1811.

[444] Wexford Catholic Meeting, 12 Sept., reported in *DEP*, 14 Sept. 1811.

[445] Hay to O'Connell, 10 Oct. 1811 in *O'Connell Correspondence Vol.1*, p.269.

[446] *DEP*, 26 Dec. 1811.

[447] Richmond to Ryder, 1 Mar. 1812, regarding Catholic meeting 28 Feb. 1812, HO 100/166/156-159.

[448] *DEP*, 25 Apr. 1812.

[449] Hay's notes *c*.1819, DDA CAP 390/2/12/12.

[450] I am grateful to MaryRose Hay and Dr Vincent Hay for allowing me to examine Hay papers in their possession. Hay's correspondents included members of the British royal family.

[451] Hay to *Carrick Morning Post*, 11 Dec. 1819.

452 Hay to O'Connell, 4 and 8 May 1812 in *O'Connell Correspondence Vol.I*, nos. 374 and 377, pp289-290, 293-294.

453 Hay to O'Connell, 30 May 1812 in *Ibid.*, no.383, pp297-298.

454 Catholic proceedings, 8 May and 23 Jun. 1812, DDA CAP 54/2/2/20 and 54/2/3/4.

455 Hay to O'Connell, 12 Sept. 1812 in *O'Connell Correspondence Vol.I*, no.392, pp305-307.

456 Hay to O'Connell, *O'Connell Correspondence, Vol.I*, 12 Sept. 1812 no.392, p.307.

457 Catholic proceedings, 26 Mar. 1812, DDA CAP 54/2/1/30.

458 Various documents, Apr. 1812, DDA CAP 390/2/6/14.

459 See chapter six for details of Hay's family and their circumstances.

460 Dromgoole to Hay, 9 May, and Richard O'Brien to Hay, 23 May 1812, DDA CAP 390/1/7/20/22.

461 Hay to Dromgoole, 14 May 1812, DDA CAP 390/1/19/31.

462 O'Connell speech at a Catholic Meeting, 2 Jul. 1812 in John O'Connell (ed.), *The Selected Speeches of Daniel O'Connell Vol.I* (Dublin, 1877), pp79-80.

463 Tim D'Arcy to Hay, 9 Nov. 1912, DDA CAP 390/2/1/29.

464 Hays circulars, 15 Oct. and 19 Dec. 1812, DDA CAP 54/2/3/20/30.

465 Hay circular to Catholic Board, 5 Oct. 1812, DDA CAP 390/2/5/6.

466 Subcommittee of accounts to James Bagot, 23 Dec. 1812, DDA CAP 390/1/20/47.

467 Burke to Hay, 10 Jan. 1812, DDA CAP 390/1/7/3.

468 Netterville to Hay, 7 Sept., and Fingall to Hay, 2 Oct. 1812, DDA CAP 390/1/7.

469 Catholic proceedings, 24 Dec. 1812, DDA CAP 54/2/3/31; Dromgoole

was nicknamed Drumsuffle according his entry in the *Dictionary of National Biography*.

470 William Tighe to Hay, 4 Apr., and Jane McAwly, 1 Aug. 1812, DDA CAP 390/1/7/7/35; Dominic Bellew to Hay, 31 Dec. 1812, DDA CAP 390/1/13/33.

471 Norman Gash, *Mr Secretary Peel* (London, 1961), p.158; Gerard O'Brien, 'Robert Peel and the Pursuit of Catholic Emancipation, 1813-17' in *Archivium Hibernicum* Vol. xliii, 1988, pp135-141.

472 *DEP*, 2 Jul. 1812.

473 Peter Bodkin-Hussey to Scully, 23 Feb. 1813 in *Scully Papers* no.405, p.427.

474 Peter Bodkin-Hussey to Scully, 1 Mar. 1813 in *Scully Papers* no.410, p.432.

475 Catholic Meetings, 2 Feb. and 13 Feb. 1813, DDA CAP 54/1/9/1/3.

476 Brian Inglis, 'O'Connell and the Irish Press 1800-42' in *IHS*, 8, 29, March 1952 pp1-27, pp4-5.

477 Connolly, 'Union Government, 1812-23' in Vaughan (ed.) *New History of Ireland*, pp48-73, p.50.

478 *DEP*, 18 May 1813.

479 *DEP*, 3 Jun. 1813.

480 *DEP*, 5 Jun. 1813.

481 Committee of accounts meeting, 21 Jun. 1813; notes by Hay, 29 Jun. 1824, DDA CAP 60/2/15/5.

482 Catholic Committee/Board accounts, 1809-13, DDA CAP 60/2/1.

483 Catholic Committee/Board accounts, 1809-13, DDA CAP 60/2/1; Arthur Aspinall, *Politics and the Press 1780-1850* (Brighton, 1973), p.321.

484 Financial Returns of the Catholic Committee/Board, 1809-13, DDA CAP 54/1/5.

485 *DEP*, 12 Jun. 1813.

486 *DEP*, 19 Oct. 1813.

487 *DEP*, 5 Mar. 1814.

488 *DEP*, 29 Jun. and 3 Jul. 1813.

489 Quarantotti was Vice-Prefect of Propaganda at the Vatican. He was willing

490 to accept British monarchical influence in the selection of Irish bishops.

490 Quarantotti Rescript, 16 Feb. 1814, DDA CAP 390/1/20/49.

491 *DEP*, 20 and 24 Jul. 1813.

492 Martin Coen, 'The Choosing of Oliver Kelly for the See of Tuam, 1809-15' in *Journal of the Galway Archaeological and Historical Society*, 1977, pp14-29, p.27.

493 Donoughmore/Hay correspondence (thirty-four letters) in Donoughmore Papers PRONI T.3459/D/16.

494 Donoughmore to Francis Hely-Hutchinson, 21 Dec. 1813 in Donoughmore Papers PRONI T.345WFI10/92.

495 Donoughmore to Hay, 26 Jan. 1814, DDA CAP 390/1/11/22.

496 Catholic Meeting, 22 Jan. 1814, DDA CAP54/1/10/3.

497 *DEP*, 5 Mar. 1814.

498 Catholic Meetings, 5, 12 and 19 Mar. and 12 Apr. 1814, DDA CAP 54/1/10/18/19/21.

499 Hay to Ffrench, 27 Jan. 1807, DDA CAP390/1/19/42.

500 Jerningham to Hay, 14 Apr. 1814, DDA CAP 390/2/1/39.

501 Donoughmore to Francis Hely-Hutchinson, 10 May 1814 in Donoughmore Papers PRONI T.34591FI10193.

502 Fingal1 to Hay, 23 Feb. 1814, DDA CAP 390/1/8/86.

503 *DEP*, 10 May 1814.

504 Thomas Wyse, *Historical Sketch of the Catholic Association* (London, 1829), p.189.

505 *DEP*, 8 Dec. 1814, quoting from the *Cork Mercantile Chronicle*.

506 *FJ*, 25 Jan. 1815.

507 *DEP*, 1 Mar. 1815.

508 Power to Bray, 3 Jan. 1815, Bray Papers, Cashel Diocesan Archives, cited in McNally, 'Archbishop Troy', p.515.

509 *DEP*, 10 Jan. 1815.

510 *DEP*, 19 Jan. 1815.

511 *Carrick Morning Post* (published in Dublin), 11 Dec. 1819.

512 *DEP*, 26 Jan. 1815.

513 *DEP*, 14 Feb. 1815.

514 *DEP*, 21 Oct. 1815, and Catholic proceedings, 29 Aug. 1815, DDA CAP 60/2/2/8.

515 David O'Callaghan to Hay, 17 Sept. and 11 Oct. 1815, DDA CAP 390/1/9/17/18.

516 Donoughmore to Hay, 9 Feb., 17 Oct. and 30 Dec. 1815, DDA CAP 390/2/4/16/25/27.

517 James O'Shaughnessy, 28 Mar. 1815, DDA CAP 390/1/9/4.

518 Fingall to Hay, 16 Mar. and 3 May 1815, DDA CAP 390/1/9/92/94.

519 Hay to Edward Hay (Ross), 29 Apr., 6 Jun. and 13 Nov. 1815, DDA CAP 390/2/5/10/12/13.

520 Cathaldus Giblin (ed.), 'Papers of Richard Joachim Hayes, OFM, 1810-1824, in Franciscan Library, Killiney' in *Collectanea Hibernica* 21-30, 1981-88.

521 Peel to Sidmouth, 17 Aug. 1816, PRO HO 100/190/133-5. My thanks to Tom Bartlett for this reference.

522 Patrick Hayes to Richard Hayes, 12 Mar. 1817 in 'Papers of Hayes' no.254 in *Collectanea Hibernica*, 26, 1985, p.92.

523 McNally, 'Archbishop Troy', p.548.

524 Hay to Donoughmore, 25 Apr. 1818 in Donoughmore papers, PRONI T.34591D/16/21.

525 Hay to Donoughmore, 19 Jul. 1816 in Donoughmore papers, PRONI T.34591D116/9.

526 O'Connell to Hay, 27 Jul. 1817 in *O'Connell Correspondence Vol.II*, no.713, pp159-160.

527 Hay's notes, 29 Jun. 1824, DDA CAP 60/2/15/55.

528 M.R. O'Connell, 'Daniel O'Connell: Income, Expenditure and Despair' in *IHS*, 17, 1970-71, pp200-220. This article clearly

explains O'Connell's haphazard financial arrangements.

[529] *DEP*, 20 Nov. 1818.

[530] Troy to Hay, 30 Nov. 1818, DDA CAP 60/2/15/9.

[531] Circular on Hay's behalf, 1 Dec. 1818, DDA CAP 60/2/5/12.

[532] O'Connell to Owen O'Conor, 21 Dec. 1818 in *O'Connell Correspondence Vol.II*, no.754, pp184-185.

[533] Hay to Bedford (undated), DDA CAP 390/2/5/14.

[534] O'Connell quoted in Madden, *History of the United Irishmen*, p.528.

[535] Catholic Meeting, 1 Mar. reported in *DEP*, 3 Mar. 1819.

[536] *DEP*, 3 Jul. 1819.

[537] Canning to Hay, 12 May 1819, DDA CAP 60/2/6/6.

[538] *DEP*, 3 Jul. 1819.

[539] Hay to *DEP*, 10 Jul. 1819.

[540] *DEP*, 17 Aug. 1819.

[541] O'Connell to *DEP*, 2 Sept. 1819.

[542] Donoughmore to Hay, 19 Jul. 1819, DDA CAP 390/2/4/28.

[543] O'Connell to Mary O'Connell, 18 Aug. 1819 in *O'Connell Correspondence Vol.I*, no.785, pp213-214.

[544] Undated letter by Hay, DDA CAP 390/2/9/12.

[545] *DEP*, 11 Nov. 1819.

[546] Undated notes by Hay (seventeen- and a-half-pages), DDA CAP 60/2/15/7.

[547] *DEP*, 2 Dec. 1819.

[548] Hay to *DEP*, 18 Dec. 1819.

[549] *DMP*, 28 Jul. 1824.

[550] *DMP*, 31 Jul. 1824. .

[551] Kilmainham Gaol Register 1/10/50 NAI (V16-6-38).

[552] Rough draft of a letter written by Hay, 29 June 1824, DDA CAP 60/2/15/4; Hay to *Saunder's Newsletter* explaining his predicament, 29 Jun. 1824, DDA CAP 60/2/15/5.

[553] *DMP*, 3 Aug. 1824.

[554] *DMP*, 11 Aug. 1824.

[555] *DMP*, 13 Jul. 1824; Hay to *DMP*, 14

[556] Aug. 1824.

[556] *DEP*, 13 Jul. 1824.

[557] *DEP*, 13 Jul. 1824.

[558] Brian Inglis, 'The Freedom of the Press in Ireland 1784-1842' (PhD, TCD, 1950), p.330; Aspinall, *Politics and the Press*, p.319.

[559] Inglis, 'Freedom of the Press in Ireland', p.330; Aspinall, *Politics and the Press*, p.330.

[560] (An army officer), 'A few observations on Mr Hay's exaggerated account of the insurrection in Wexford' (1833), Ms insert in Joly copy (NL1) of Hay's *History* (1803).

[561] Hay to *DEP*, 29 Jan. 1822.

[562] Hay to *DEP*, 7 Feb. 1822.

[563] O'Connell to Hay, 27 July 1817 in *O'Connell Correspondence Vol.II*, pp159-60.

[564] JKL to *DEP*, 21 Mar. 1822.

[565] Fitzpatrick, *Life, Letters and Correspondence Vol.I*, p.187.

[566] Hay to JKL, 25 Jun. 1824 in Bishop's House, Carlow College.

[567] Hay to *DEP*, 21 Feb. 1822

[568] Hay, 'History of the Catholics', undated but probably 1822, DDA CAP 54/2/5.

[569] *Ibid.*

[570] *Ibid.*

[571] Hay to JKL, 25 Jun. 1824 in Bishop's House, Carlow.

[572] I am indebted to the Maher family for this information and access to a lease for Ballinkeele House dated 1807.

[573] R.R. Madden, *History of the United Irishmen*, p.532.

[574] Information courtesy of the Maher family, Ballinkeele House.

[575] Deed dated 11 Jun. 1825 in the Registry of Deeds, Dublin 803 (510) 542245. This document suggests that both Philip and Edward Hay were defendants.

[576] Hay's Family 1826, DDA CAP 60/2/18/5. I am grateful to Mary-

Rose Hay, who provided me with the name of her ancestor James Hay. He served in the Royal Irish Constabulary. She also passed on information on Winifred Hay, who died in 1840, see *Wexford Independent*, 25 Apr. 1840. Bill Sweetman unearthed this death notice.

577 *Wexford Evening Post*, 20 Oct. 1826.

578 Catholic Association Minutes, 14 Oct. 1826 in NAI Catholic Association Papers, box 1160; *Gentleman's Magazine and History Chronicle*, 96, 11 Jul., Dec. 1826, p.477.

579 *FJ*, 19 Oct. 1826.

580 *DEP*, 17 Oct. 1826.

581 Catholic Association Minutes, 14 Oct. 1826 in NAI Catholic Association Papers, box 1160.

582 Hay Family, DDA CAP 60/2/18/5.

583 *FJ*, 24 Apr. 1840, my thanks to Bill Sweetman for this reference; Madden, *History of the United Irishmen*, pp524-9, 532.

584 My thanks to the talented fifth-year students in St Louis Secondary School, Carrickmacross, County Monaghan, from whom I learnt so much about *Othello* in 1992-93.

585 For a sample, see Ciaran Brady (ed.), *Losers in Irish History* (Dublin, 1985).

586 Elliott, *Wolfe Tone*, p.138, 170.

587 *Ibid.*, p.171.

588 *Ibid.*, p.232.

589 D.G. Boyce, *Nationalism in Ireland* (London, 1982), p.132; K.T. Hoppen, *Ireland Since 1800: Conflict and Conformity* (New York, 1989), p.16

590 Thomas Wyse, *Historical Sketch of the late Catholic Association of Ireland, Vol.I* (London, 1829), p.155.

591 Peter Jupp, 'Irish Parliamentary Elections and the Influence of the Catholic Vote, 1801-20' in *The Historical Journal* 10, 2, 1967, pp183-196, p.196.

592 Hay to Litta, 15 Aug. 1817 in *DEP*, 26 Jan. 1822.

593 Kevin Whelan, 'The Catholic Community in eighteenth century County Wexford' in Power & Whelan (eds), *Endurance and Emergence*, pp129-170, p.158.

594 Hoppen, *Conflict and Conformity*, p.15.

595 R.F. Foster, *Modern Ireland 1600-1972* (London, 1988), p.298.

596 A.T.Q. Stewart, 'A Stable Unseen Power: Dr William Drennan and the Origins of the United Irishmen' in John Bossy & Peter Jupp (eds), *Essays Presented to Michael Roberts* (Belfast, 1976), pp80-92.

597 Cited in Fitzpatrick, *JKL* Vol.I, p.180.

598 Grattan, *Life Vol. V*, p.403, 441.

599 Fingall to O'Connell, 27 Feb. 1810 in *O'Connell Correspondence Vol.I*, no.270, p.214.

600 W.J. Fitzpatrick (ed.), *Correspondence of Daniel O'Connell Vol.II* (London, 1880), p.57.

601 O'Connell quoted in R.R. Madden, *History of the United Irishmen*, p.528.

BIBLIOGRAPHY

❦

PRIMARY

MANUSCRIPTS

Dublin Diocesan Archives:
Catholic Association Papers, 54/1, 54/2, 55/3, 60/2, 390/1 and 390/2.
Troy Correspondence.

National Archives of Ireland:
Catholic Association Papers, box 1160.
Frazer Ms.
Kilmainham Gaol Register 1/10/50 (V16-6-38).
Rebellion Papers, 620.

National Library of Ireland, Manuscripts Department:
Barton Ms 5637.
Brownrigg, John, 'Letter on 1798' Ms 27/485(3), p[hotostat] 7.
Handcock, Thomas, 'Narrative of the Battle of Enniscorthy on 28 May 1798' Ms
    16,232, p[hotostat] 37.
HO 100 (on microfilm).
Minute Books of the Irish Catholic Committee I (May 1809-August 1810), II
    (August 1810-June 1811) Ms 4321-4322.
Percy Ms 4157.

National Library of Ireland, Prints and Drawings:
Christopher Taylor, Printer, Wexford.

Public Record Office of Northern Ireland:
Donoughmore Papers T3459.
McPeake Papers T3048.
Pelham Papers T755.

Registry of Deeds, Dublin:
Deed dated 11 June 1825 in the 803 (510) 542245.

Royal Irish Academy:
Burrowes Ms 23 K53.

Sheffield City Archives:
Fitzwilliam Papers

St Kieran's College, Kilkenny:
Dowling Papers.

St Patrick's, Carlow College:
Hay Correspondence with James Warren Doyle, Bishop of Kildare and Leighlin.

Trinity College, Dublin, Manuscripts Department:
Musgrave Depositions, Ms 871.
Sirr Papers, Ms 896.

MANUSCRIPTS IN PRIVATE HANDS:

Correspondence of the Hay family courtesy of William Sweetman, Wexford.
Hay family papers courtesy of Maryrose Hay, Wicklow and Dr Vincent Hay, Canada.
Ballinkeele papers courtesy of the Maher family, Ballinkeele House, County Wexford.

PRINTED

(An army officer), 'A few observations on Mr Hay's exaggerated account of the in-
surrection in Wexford' (1833), Ms in NLI Joly copy of Hay, *History* (Dublin 1803).
'Case of Captain Philip Hay, 1798: A Narrative of the Proceedings of the Commis-
sioners of Suffering Loyalists in the Case of Captain Philip Hay, of the 18th Light
Dragoons, with Remarks thereon by George, Earl of Kingston' in *Cork Historical
and Archaeological Society Journal* 10, 1904, pp190-204.
Barrington, Jonah, *Rise and Fall of the Irish Nation* (Paris, 1833).
Bartlett, Thomas (ed.), 'Select Documents XXXVIII: Defenders and Defenderism
in 1795' in IHS, 24, 95, May 1985, pp372-294.
Beatty, John D. (ed.), *Protestant women's narratives of the Irish rebellion of 1798* (Dublin, 2001).
Bushe, G.P. 'An Essay towards ascertaining the population of Ireland' in *Transactions
of the Royal Irish Academy, Vol III*, 1789-90, pp145-55.
Byrne, Miles, *Memoirs of Miles Byrne* (Shannon, 1972).
Cloney, Thomas, *A Personal Narrative of those Transactions in the County in which the
Author was Engaged* (Dublin, 1832).
Fitzpatrick, W.J. (ed), *Correspondence of Daniel O'Connell Vol II* (London, 1880).
Fitzpatrick, W.J. (ed.), *Lives, Letters and Correspondence of Dr Doyle (JKL) Bishop of
Kildare and Leighlin Vol I* (Dublin, 1880).
Giblin, Cathadus (ed.), 'Papers of Richard Joachim Hayes, OFM, 1810-1824, in Fran-
ciscan Library, Killiney' in *Collectanea Hibernica* 21-30, 1981-88.
Gordon, J.B., *History of the Rebellion in the Year 1798* 2nd ed. (Dublin, 1803).
Hay, Edward, *History of the Insurrection of County Wexford AD 1798* (Dublin, 1803).
Hay, *History*, NLI Joly copy (Dublin, 1803).
Hay, *History* (Dublin, 1842).
Hay, *History* (Dublin, 1847).
Hay, *History* (Dublin, 1898).
Hay, *History* (New York, 1873).
Hay, *History* published with Michael Doherty, *The History of the American Revolution*
(Dublin, 1848).
Historical Manuscripts Commission (Donoughmore) 12th Report.
Historical Manuscripts Commission Report on the Manuscript of J.B. Fortescue Vol 9, 1915.
MacDermot, Brian (ed.), *The Catholic Question in England and Ireland: The Papers of
Denys Scully 1798-1822* (Dublin, 1988).

MacDermot, Brian (ed.) *The Irish Catholic Petition of 1805: the diary of Denys Scully* (Dublin, 1992).

Malcomson, A.P.W. (ed.), *Eighteenth Century Irish Official Papers in Great Britain Private Collections: Vol I* (Belfast, 1973).

Malcomson, A.P.W. (ed.) *An Anglo-Irish Dialogue. A Calendar of the Correspondence between John Foster and Lord Sheffield 1774-1821* (Belfast, 1975).

Malcomson, A.P.W. (ed.), *Eighteenth Century Irish Official Papers in Great Britain. Private Collections Vol II* (Belfast, 1990).

McDowell, R.B. (ed.), *Correspondence of Edmund Burke 1794-96 Vol VIII* (Chicago, 1969).

Musgrave, Richard, *Memoirs of the Different Rebellions in Ireland* (Dublin, 1801).

Myers, Steven & Dolores E. McKnight (eds), *Memoirs of the Different Rebellions in Ireland, by Sir Richard Musgrave, Bart.* (Fort Wayne, 1995).

Newenham, Thomas, *A Statistical and Historical Inquiry into the Progress and Magnitude of the Population of Ireland* (London, 1805).

NLI Reports on Private Collections No.261.

O'Connell, John (ed.), *The Selected Speeches of Daniel O'Connell Vol I* (Dublin, 1877).

O'Connell, M.R. (ed.), *The Correspondence of Daniel O'Connell 8 Vols* (Shannon, 1972-81).

Plowden, Francis, *An Historical Review of the State of Ireland from the Invasion of that Country under Henry II to its Union with Great Britain Vol II* (London, 1803).

Taylor, George, *A History of the Rise, Progress, Cruelties and Suppression of the Rebellion in the County of Wexford* (Dublin, 1800).

Teeling, C.H., *History of the Irish Rebellion of 1798* (Shannon, 1972).

Todd Jones, William, *A Letter to the Societies of United Irishmen of the town of Belfast* (Dublin, 1792).

Wakefield, Edward, *An Account of Ireland, Statistical and Political Vol II* (London, 1812).

Woods, C.C. & R.E. Ward (eds), *The Letters of Charles O'Conor of Belanagare 2 Vols* (Ann Arbor, 1980).

Wyse, Thomas, *Historical Sketch of the Catholic Association* (London, 1829).

NEWSPAPERS
Carrick Morning Post
Cork Mercantile Chronicle
Dublin Evening Post
Faulkiner's Dublin Journal
Freeman's Journal
Gentleman's Magazine and History Chronicle
Saunder's Newsletter
Wexford Evening Post
Wexford Independent

PERIODICALS
Watty Cox's *Irish Magazine*
Wolfe Tone Annual

SECONDARY

Andrews, J.H., 'Landmarks in Early Wexford Cartography' in Whelan (ed.), *Wexford*, pp447-466.

Anon., 'Students of the Irish College Salamanca (1595-1619)' in *Archivium Hibernicum* 2, 1913, p.29.

Aspinall, Arthur, *Politics and the Press 1780-1850* (Brighton, 1973).

Bartlett, Thomas, '"A weapon of war, yet untried": Irish Catholics and the armed forces of the crown' in T.J. Fraser & Keith Jeffery (eds), *Men, Women and War: Historical Studies XVIII* (Dublin, 1993), pp66-85.

Bartlett, Thomas, 'An End to Moral Economy. The Irish Militia Disturbances of 1793' in *Past and Present* 99, 1983, pp41-64.

Bartlett, Thomas, 'Defence, counter-insurgency and rebellion: Ireland, 1793-1803' in Thomas Bartlett & Keith Jeffery (eds), *A Military History of Ireland* (Cambridge, 1996) pp247-294.

Bartlett, Thomas, 'Miles Byrne: United Irishman, Irish Exile and Beau Sabreur' in Keogh & Furlong (eds), *The Mighty Wave*, pp118-138.

Bartlett, Thomas, 'Protestant nationalism in eighteenth-century Ireland' in Michael O'Dea & Kevin O'Dea (eds), *Nations and Nationalisms: France, Britain and Ireland in the eighteenth-century context* (Oxford, 1995), pp79-88.

Bartlett, Thomas, 'Religious rivalries in France and Ireland in the age of the French Revolution' in *Eighteenth-Century Ireland, Iris an dá chultúr*, 6, 1991, pp57-76.

Bartlett, Thomas, 'Review of *A New History of Ireland*' in *Past and Present* No.116, 1987, pp206-219.

Bartlett, Thomas, 'Why the history of the 1798 rebellion has yet to be written', *Eighteenth-Century Ireland* Vol.15, 2000, pp178-187.

Bartlett, Thomas & Keith Jeffery (eds), *A Military History of Ireland* (Cambridge, 1996).

Bartlett, Thomas, *The Fall and Rise of the Irish Nation. The Catholic Question in Ireland, 1690-1830* (Dublin, 1992).

Bartlett, Thomas, David Dickson, Dáire Keogh & Kevin Whelan (eds), *1798, A Bicentenary Perspective* (Dublin, 2003).

Bergeron, Paul & L.M. Cullen (eds), *Culture et Pratiques Politiques en France et en Irlande XVIe-XVIIIe* (Paris, 1991).

Betham, *Prerogative Marriage Abstracts Series IV Vol.8*, 1753-1800.

Birch, Peter, *St Kieran's College Kilkenny* (Dublin, 1951).

Boyce, D.G., *Nationalism in Ireland* (London, 1982).

Boyce, D.G., *Nineteenth Century: The Search for Stability: New Gill History of Ireland Vol V* (Dublin, 1990).

Brady, Ciaran (ed.), *Losers in Irish History* (Dublin, 1985).

Brown, Michael, Patrick Geoghegan & James Kelly (eds), *The Irish Act of Union, 1800. Bicentennial Essays* (Dublin, 2003).

Bull, Philip, Frances Devlin-Glass & Helen Doyle (eds), *Ireland and Australia, 1798-1998. Studies in Culture, Identity and Migration* (Sydney, 2000).

Butel, Paul & L.M. Cullen (eds), *French and Irish Perspectives on Urban Development, 1500-1900* (Dublin, 1988).

Clifford, Brenda, Brid Finnegan, Geraldine Gallagher & Mary Murphy, 'Duelling in early nineteenth-century Ireland' in *Retrospect: Journal of the Irish History Students' Association* 1989, pp1-8.

Cloney, Sean, 'The Cloney Families of County Wexford' in Whelan, *Wexford*, pp316-341.

Coen, Martin, 'The Choosing of Oliver Kelly for the See of Tuam, 1809-15' in *Journal of the Galway Archaeological and Historical Society*, 1977, pp14-29.

Comerford, Vincent, 'Daniel O'Connell' in *Oxford Dictionary of National Biography*.

Connolly, Claire, 'Completing the Union? The Irish Novel and the Moment of Union' in Michael Brown, Patrick M. Egghead & James Kelly (eds), *The Irish Act of Union, 1800* (Dublin, 2003), pp157-175.

Connolly, S.J. (ed.), *The Oxford Companion to Irish History* (Oxford, 1998).

Connolly, S.J., 'The Catholic Question, 1801-12' in W.E. Vaughan (ed.), *A New History of Ireland, Volume V: Ireland Under the Union I, 1801-1870* (Oxford, 1989), pp24-47.

Corish, P.J., *The Catholic Community in the Seventeenth and Eighteenth Centuries* (Dublin, 1981).

Corish, Patrick, 'Two centuries of Catholicism in County Wexford' in Kevin Whelan (ed), *Wexford: History and Society*, pp222-247.

Cullen, L.M., 'Late Eighteenth-Century Politicisation in Ireland: Problems in its Study and its French Links' in Bergeron & Cullen (eds), *Culture et Pratique Politiques*, pp137-157.

Cullen, L.M., 'The 1798 Rebellion in its Eighteenth-Century Context' in P.J. Corish (ed.), *Radicals, Rebels and Establishment: Historical Studies XV* (Belfast, 1985), pp91-113.

Cullen, L.M., 'The 1798 Rebellion in Wexford: United Irishman Organisation, Membership and Leadership' in Kevin Whelan (ed.), *Wexford: History and Society* (Dublin, 1987), pp222-247.

Cullen, L.M. 'The Dublin Merchant Community in the Eighteenth Century' in Paul Butel & L.M. Cullen (eds), *French and Irish Perspectives on Urban Development, 1500-1900* (Dublin, 1988), pp95-209.

Cullen, L.M., *The Emergence of Modern Ireland* (London, 1981).

Cullen, Mary, Vincent Comerford, Jacqueline Hill & Colm Lennon (eds), *Religion, Conflict and Coexistence* (Dublin, 1989).

De Brún, Pádraig, 'The Irish Society's Bible Teachers, 1818-27' in *Éigse, A Journal of Irish Studies*, xix, part II, 1983, pp281-332.

Dickson, Charles, *The Wexford Rising, Its Causes and its Course* (Tralee, 1955).

Dickson, David, 'Foreword' in Steven W. Myers & Dolores E. McKnight (eds), *Memoirs of the Different Rebellions in Ireland, by Sir Richard Musgrave, Bart.* (Fort Wayne, 1995), ppi-xiii.

Dickson, David, *New Foundations: Ireland 1660-1800* (Dublin, 2000, second revised and enlarged edition).

Dickson, David, Cormac Ó Gráda and Stuart Daultrey, 'Hearth Tax, Household Size and Irish Population Change 1672-1821' in *Proceedings of the Royal Irish Academy*, 82c, 1982, pp125-81.

Dickson, David & Cormac Ó Gráda (eds), *Refiguring Ireland. Essays in Honour of L.M. Cullen* (Dublin, 2003).

Donald, Aileen, 'John Keogh: The Pursuit of Catholic Emancipation 1780-1795' (MA thesis, St Patrick's College, DCU, 1999).

Donnelly, James S. Jr, 'Sectarianism in 1798 and in Catholic nationalist memory' in Lawrence Geary (ed.), *Rebellion and Remembrance in Modern Ireland*.

Duffy, Eamon, 'Ecclesiastical Democracy Detected: 1 (1779-1787)' in *Recusant History* 10, 4, Jan. 1970, pp193-209.

Dunne, Thomas, 'Representations of Rebellion; 1798 in Literature' in F.B. Smith (ed.), *Ireland, England and Australia* (Canberra and Cork, 1990), pp14-40.

Dunne, Tom, *Rebellions. Memoir, Memory and 1798* (Dublin, 2004).

Elliott, Marianne, 'Wolfe Tone and the Development of a Revolutionary Culture in Ireland' in Bergeron & Cullen (eds), *Culture et Pratique Politiques*, pp171-186.

Elliott, Marianne, *Wolfe Tone. Prophet of Irish Independence* (New Haven and London, 1989).

Foster, R.F. (ed.), *The Oxford Illustrated History of Ireland* (Oxford, 1989).

Foster, R.F., 'Ascendancy and Union' in R.F. Foster (ed.), *The Oxford Illustrated History of Ireland* (Oxford, 1989), pp161-22.

Foster, R.F., *Modern Ireland 1600-1972* (London, 1988).

Foster, R.F. *Paddy and Mr Punch. Connections in Irish and English History* (London, 1993).

Furlong, Nicholas & John Hayes, *County Wexford in the Rare Oul' Times Vol II* (Wexford, 1987).

Furlong, Nicholas, *Fr Murphy of Boolavogue, 1753-1798* (Dublin, 1991).

Gahan, Daniel, 'Class, religion and rebellion: Wexford in 1798' in Jim Smyth (ed.), *Revolution, counter-revolution and union* (Cambridge, 2000), pp82-98.

Gahan, Daniel, *The People's Rising. The Wexford Rebellion of 1798* (Dublin, 1995).

Gash, Norman, *Mr Secretary Peel* (London, 1961).

Geary, Lawrence M. (ed.), *Rebellion and remembrance in modern Ireland* (Dublin, 2001).

Geoghegan, Patrick, *Lord Castlereagh* (Dundalk, 2002).

Geoghegan, Patrick, *The Irish Act of Union* (Dublin, 1999).

Gilbert, J.T. & Margaret Ó hÓgartaigh, 'Edward Hay' in Matthew, H.C.G. & Brian Harrison (eds), *Oxford Dictionary of National Biography Vol. 25* (Oxford, 2004), pp991-2.

Gough, Hugh & David Dickson (eds), *Ireland and the French Revolution* (Dublin, 1990).

Grattan, Henry (Jr), *Memoirs of the Right Honourable Henry Grattan Vol V* (London, 1849).

Hague, William, *William Pitt the Younger* (London, 2005).

Hehir, Irene, 'New Lights and Old Enemies: The "Second Reformation" and the Catholics of Ireland, 1800-1835' (MA, University of Wisconsin, 1983).

Hempton, David, 'The Methodist Crusade in Ireland 1795-1845', IHS, 22, 85, March 1980, pp33-48.

Hempton, David, 'Wesleyan Methodism and Educational Politics in Early Nineteenth-century England' in *History of Education*, Vol. 8, No. 3, 1979, pp207-221.

Hill, Jacqueline, 'Popery and Protestantism, Civil and Religious Liberty: The Disputed Lessons of Irish History 1690-1812' in *Past and Present*, 118, 1988, pp96-129.

Hill, Jacqueline, 'Dublin After the Union: The Age of the Ultra Protestants, 1801-22' in Michael Brown, Patrick Egghead & James Kelly (eds), *The Irish Act of Union, 1800. Bicentennial Essays* (Dublin, 2003), pp144-56.

Hogan, Edmund, *The Description of Ireland and the State thereof as it is at this time present in Anno 1598* (Dublin, 1879).

Hoppen, K.T., *Ireland Since 1800: Conflict and Conformity* (New York, 1989).

Hore, Philip, *History of the Town of Wexford Vol. IV* (London, 1900-1906).

Inglis, Brian, 'O'Connell and the Irish Press 1800-42' in *IHS*, 8, 29, March 1952, pp1-27.

Inglis, Brian, 'The Freedom of the Press in Ireland 1784-1842' (PhD, TCD, 1950).

Jeffrey, W.H., *Castles of Wexford* (Wexford, 1979).

Johnston, E.M., 'Problems Common to both Protestant and Catholic Churches in Eighteenth-Century Ireland' in Oliver MacDonagh, W.F. Mandle & Pauric Travers (eds), *Irish Culture and Nationalism, 1750-1950* (London, 1983), pp14-39.

Joyce, John, *General Thomas Cloney: Wexford Rebel of 1798* (Dublin, 1988).

Jupp, Peter, 'Dr Duigenan reconsidered' in Sabine Wichert (ed.), *From the United Irishmen to Twentieth-Century Unionism* (Dublin, 2004), pp79-96.

Jupp, Peter, 'Irish Parliamentary Elections and the Influence of the Catholic Vote, 1801-20' in *The Historical Journal* 10, 2, 1967, pp183-196.

Jupp, Peter, *Lord Grenville 1759-1834* (Oxford, 1985).

Kavanagh, P.F., *A Popular History of the Insurrection of 1798* (Cork, 1898).

Kelly, James, *Sir Richard Musgrave, 1746-1818, Ultra- Protestant Ideologue* (Dublin, 2009).

Kelly, James, 'John Keogh' in *Oxford DNB Vol 31*, pp356-357.

Kelly, James, 'Popular Politics in Ireland and the Act of Union' in *Transactions of the Royal Historical Society, Sixth Series, X* (Cambridge, 2000), pp259-287.

Kelly, James, *'That Damn'd Thing Called Honour'. Duelling in Ireland 1570-1860* (Cork, 1995).

Kelly, James, 'The Parliamentary Reform Movement of the 1790s and the Catholic Question' in *Archivium Hibernicum* 42, 1988, pp95-117.

Kelly, James & Dáire Keogh (eds), *History of the Catholic Diocese of Dublin* (Dublin, 2000).

Keogh, Dáire, '"The pattern of the flock": John Thomas Troy, 1786-1823' in James Kelly & Dáire Keogh (eds), *History of the Catholic Diocese of Dublin* (Dublin, 2000), pp215-236.

Keogh, Dáire, *'The French Disease': the Catholic Church and Radicalism in Ireland, 1790-1800* (Dublin, 1993).

Kinsella, Anna, '1798 Claimed for the Catholics: Father Kavanagh, Fenians and the Centenary Celebrations' in Keogh & Furlong (eds), *The Mighty Wave*, pp139-155.

Kleinrichert, Denise, *Republican Internment and the Prison Ship Argenta, 1922* (Dublin, 2001).

Lee, J.J., *The Population of Ireland before the 19th Century* (London, 1973).

Leighton, C.D.A., 'Gallicanism and the Veto Controversy: Church, State and Catholic Community in early Nineteenth-Century Ireland' in Mary Cullen, Vincent Comerford, Jacqueline Hill & Colm Lennon (eds), *Religion, Conflict and Coexistence* (Dublin, 1989), pp135-158.

McGuire, James & James Quinn (eds), *Dictionary of Irish Biography* (Cambridge, 2009).

MacDonagh, Oliver, 'The Politicisation of Irish Catholic Bishops, 1800-1850' in *Historical Journal* 18, 1975, pp37-53.

MacDonagh, Oliver, *O'Connell: The Life of Daniel O'Connell, 1775-1847* (London, 1991).

MacSuibhne, Peadar, *'98 in Carlow* (Carlow, 1974).

Madden, R.R., *The Lives of the United Irishmen Vol IV 4th series* (Dublin, 1860).

Mannion, John, 'A Transatlantic Merchant Fishery: Richard Welsh of New Ross and the Sweetmans of Newfoundland 1734-1862 in Kevin Whelan (ed.), *Wexford: History and Society*, pp373-421.

Matthew, H.C.G. & Brian Harrison (eds), *Oxford Dictionary of National Biography* (Oxford, 2004).

McCartney, Donal, 'Writings on Irish History in the Early Nineteenth Century: A Study in Irish Public Opinion 1800-1830' (MA thesis, UCD, 1954).

McDowell, R.B., *Ireland in the Age of Imperialism and Revolution* (Oxford, 1979).

McGeehin, Maureen [later Wall], 'The Activities and Personnel of the General Committee of the Catholic of Ireland 1767-1784' (MA thesis, UCD, 1952).

McNally, V.J., 'Archbishop Troy and the Catholic Church in Ireland, 1789-1817' (PhD, TCD, 1977).

McNally, V.J., *Reform, revolution and reaction; Archbishop John Thomas Troy and the Catholic Church in Ireland 1787-1817* (Lantham, 1995).

Murphy, David, 'Lord Kingsborough' in *Dictionary of Irish Biography* (Cambridge, 2009).

Murphy, Hilary, *Families of Wexford* (Wexford, 1986).

Murtagh, Harman, 'Irish Soldiers Abroad, 1600-1800' in Bartlett & Jeffery (eds), *A Military History of Ireland*, pp294-314.

Nelson, Ivan, '"The first chapter of 1798"? Restoring a military perspective to the Irish Militia riots of 1793' in *IHS*, 33, 132, November 2003, pp369-386.

Nolan, William (ed.) & T.G. McGrath (associate ed.), *Tipperary: History and Society* (Dublin, 1985).

Ó hÓgartaigh, Ciarán & Ó hÓgartaigh, Margaret, 'Hedge Schools and Pre-Professional Business Education in Eighteenth-Century Ireland' in Felix Larkin (ed.), *Librarians, Poets and Scholars: a Festschrift for Dónall Ó Luanaigh* (Dublin and Portland, 2007).

Ó hÓgartaigh, Margaret, 'Edward Hay: historian of 1798' in *Eighteenth-Century Ireland, Iris an dá chultúr*, 1998, Vol.13, pp121-134.

Ó hÓgartaigh, Margaret, 'Edward Hay, Wexford Historian of 1798' in *Journal of the Wexford Historical Society* no.17, 1998-99, pp159-175.

Ó hÓgartaigh, Margaret, 'Making History and Defining the Nation: Nineteenth-century interpretations of 1798' in Philip Bull, Frances Devlin-Glass & Helen Doyle (eds), *Ireland and Australia, 1798-1998. Studies in Culture, Identity and Migration* (Sydney, 2000), pp24-33.

Ó hÓgartaigh, Margaret, 'Lord Fingall of Killeen Castle and Edward Hay of Wexford: Catholic Politics in the late eighteenth and early nineteenth century' in *Ríocht na Midhe, Records of the Meath Archaeological and Historical Society*, Vol.xviii, 2007, pp151-155.

Ó hÓgartaigh, Margaret, 'Edward Hay' in James McGuire & James Quinn (eds), *Dictionary of Irish Biography* (Cambridge, 2009).

O'Brien, Gerard (ed.), *Catholic Ireland in the Eighteenth Century – the Collected Essays of Maureen Wall* (Dublin, 1989).

O'Brien, Gerald, 'The Beginning of the Veto Controversy in Ireland' in *Journal of Ecclesiastical History* 38, 1, 1987, pp80-94.

O'Brien, Gerard, 'Robert Peel and the Pursuit of Catholic Emancipation, 1813-17' in *Archivium Hibernicum*, Vol.xliii, 1988, pp135-141.

O'Brien, Gillian, 'Camden and the move towards Union' in Dáire Keogh and Kevin Whelan (eds), *Acts of Union. The causes, contexts, and consequences of the Act of Union* (Dublin, 2001), pp106-125.

O'Brien, Gillian, 'Lord Camden in Ireland, 1795-8: A Study in Anglo-Irish Relations' (PhD, University of Liverpool, 2002).

O'Connell, M.R., 'Daniel O'Connell: Income, Expenditure and Despair' in *IHS*, 17, 1970-71, pp200-220.

O'Dea, Michael & Kevin Whelan (eds), *Nations and Nationalisms: France, Britain and Ireland in the eighteenth-century context* (Oxford, 1995).

O'Donnell, Ruán, 'Edward Fitzgerald of Newpark' in *Journal of the Wexford Historical Society* 1998-99, 17, pp121-143.

O'Donnell, Ruán, 'General Holt and the Historians' in Bob Reece (ed.), *Irish Convicts: The Origins of Convicts Transported to America* (Dublin, 1989).

O'Donnell, Ruán, *Robert Emmet and the Rising of 1803* (Dublin, 2003).

O'Donoghue, Patrick, 'The Catholic Church in an Age of Revolution and Rebellion, 1782-1803' (PhD, UCD, 1975).

O'Flaherty, Eamon, 'Irish Catholics and the French Revolution' in Hugh Gough & David Dickson (eds), *Ireland and the French Revolution*, pp52-67.

O'Flaherty, Eamon, 'The Catholic Convention and Anglo-Irish Politics, 1791-3' in *Archivium Hibernicum*, 40, 1985, pp14-34.

O'Flaherty, Eamon, 'The Catholic Question in Ireland 1774-1793' (MA thesis, UCD, 1981).

O'Hart, J.H., *The Irish and Anglo-Irish Landed Gentry* (Shannon, 1969).

O'Higgins, Fergus, 'Catholic Association Papers in the Dublin Diocesan Archives' in *Archivium Hibernicum*, 36, 1984, pp58-61.

Osborough, W.N., 'Legal aspects of the 1798 rising, its suppression and the aftermath' in Thomas Bartlett, David Dickson, Dáire Keogh & Kevin Whelan (eds), *1798*, pp 437-468.

Pakenham, Thomas, *The Year of Liberty: The Great Irish Rebellion of 1798* (London, 1969).

Powell, Thomas, 'An Economic Factor in the Wexford Rebellion of 1798' in *Studia Hibernica*, 16, 1976, pp140-157.

Powell, Thomas, 'The Background to the Rebellion in County Wexford, 1790-98' (MA thesis, UCD, 1970).

Power, T.P. & Kevin Whelan (eds), *Endurance and Emergence. Catholic in Eighteenth-Century Ireland* (Dublin, 1990).

Smith, F.B. (ed.), *Ireland, England and Australia* (Canberra and Cork, 1990).

Smyth, James, 'Popular Politicisation in Ireland in the 1790s' (PhD, Cambridge, 1989).

Smyth, James, *The men of no property: Irish radicals and popular politics in the late eighteenth century* (Dublin, 1992).

Smyth, Jim (ed.), *Revolution, counter-revolution and union* (Cambridge, 2000).

Smyth, P.D., 'The Volunteers and Parliament' in Thomas Bartlett & David Hayton (eds), *Penal Era and Golden Age* (Belfast, 1979), pp113-136.

Stewart, A.T.Q., 'A Stable Unseen Power: Dr William Drennan and the Origins of the United Irishmen' in John Bossy & Peter Jupp (eds), *Essays Presented to Michael Roberts* (Belfast, 1976), pp80-92.

Todd, Janet, *Rebel Daughters. Ireland in conflict 1798* (London, 2003).

Vaughan, W.E. (ed.), *A New History of Ireland, Volume V: Ireland Under the Union I, 1801-1870* (Oxford, 1989).

Wall, Maureen, 'The Rise of a Catholic Middle Class in Eighteenth-Century Ireland' in *IHS*, 11, 42, 1958, pp91-115.

Wall, Maureen, 'The Whiteboys' in T. Desmond Williams (ed.), *Secret Societies in Ireland* (Dublin, 1973), pp13-25.

Whelan, Kevin (ed.), *A History of Newbawn* (Newbawn, 1986).

Whelan, Kevin (ed.), *Wexford: History and Society* (Dublin, 1987).

Whelan, Kevin, 'Catholic Mobilisation, 1750-1850' in Paul Bergeron & L.M. Cullen (eds), *Culture et Pratiques Politiques en France et en Irlande XVIe-XVIIIe* (Paris, 1991), pp235-258.

Whelan, Kevin, 'Catholics, Politicisation and the 1798 Rebellion' in Reamonn Ó Muirí (ed.), *Irish Church History Today* (Armagh, 1991), pp63-83.

Whelan, Kevin, 'Interpreting the 1798 Rebellion in County Wexford' in Keogh & Furlong (eds), *The Mighty Wave*, pp9-36.

Whelan, Kevin, 'Politicisation in County Wexford and the Origins of the 1798 Rebellion' in Gough & Dickson (eds), *Ireland and the French Revolution*, pp156-178.

Whelan, Kevin, 'The Catholic Church in County Tipperary, 1700-1900' in William Nolan (ed.) & T.G. McGrath (associate ed.), *Tipperary: History and Society* (Dublin, 1985), pp215-255.

Whelan, Kevin, 'The Catholic Community in Eighteenth-Century County Wexford' in Power, T.P. & Kevin Whelan (eds), *Endurance and Emergence. Catholics in Eighteenth-Century Ireland* (Dublin, 1990), pp121-170.

Whelan, Kevin, 'The Catholic Parish, the Catholic Chapel and Village Development in Ireland in *Irish Geography* 1983, pp1-15.

Whelan, Kevin, *The Tree of Liberty. Radicalism, Catholicism and the Construction of Irish Identity, 1760-1830* (Cork, 1996).

Wichert, Sabine (ed.), *From the United Irishmen to Twentieth-Century Unionism* (Dublin, 2004).

Williams, T. Desmond (ed.), *Secret Societies in Ireland* (Dublin, 1973).

Woods, C.J., 'R.R. Madden, historian of the United Irishmen' in Bartlett, Dickson, Keogh & Whelan (eds), *1798*, pp497-511.

Woods, C.J., 'The personnel of the Catholic Convention, 1792-3' in *Archivium Hibernicum* 57, 2003, pp26-76.

Woods, C.J., 'The social composition of the Catholic Convention, 1792-3' in David Dickson & Cormac Ó Gráda (eds), *Refiguring Ireland. Essays in Honour of L.M. Cullen* (Dublin, 2003), pp165-171.

INDEX